VERTICAL COORDINATION

IN HOG PRODUCTION

by

Marvin L. Hayenga
V. J. Rhodes
Glenn A. Grimes
John D. Lawrence

| United States Department of Agriculture | Packers and Stockyards Programs | Grain Inspection, Packers and Stockyards Administration |

GIPSA-RR 96-5

May 1996

PREFACE

Congress included $500,000 in the U.S. Department of Agriculture's (USDA) Packers and Stockyards Administration (now Grain Inspection, Packers and Stockyards Administration (GIPSA) 1992 fiscal-year appropriation to conduct a study of concentration in the red meat packing industry. GIPSA solicited public comments on how to conduct the study and formed an interagency working group to advise the Agency on the study. Based on public input and comments of the working group, GIPSA selected seven projects and contracted with university researchers for six of them.

The findings of the study are summarized in Packers and Stockyards Programs, GIPSA, USDA, *Concentration in the Red Meat Packing Industry*, February 1996. The technical reports of the contractors are published as a series of Grain Inspection, Packers and Stockyards Administration Research Reports (GIPSA-RR). The technical reports of the contractors are:

GIPSA-RR 96-1	Marvin L. Hayenga, Stephen R. Koontz, and Ted C. Schroeder, *Definition of Regional Cattle Procurement Markets*.
GIPSA-RR 96-2	Slaughter Cattle Procurement and Pricing Team, Texas A&M Agricultural Market Research Center, *Price Determination in Slaughter Cattle Procurement*.
GIPSA-RR 96-3	Clement E. Ward, Ted C. Schroeder, Andrew P. Barkley, and Stephen R. Koontz, *Role of Captive Supplies in Beef Packing*.
GIPSA-RR 96-4	S. Murthy Kambhampaty, Paul Driscoll, Wayne D. Purcell, and Everett D. Peterson, *Effects of Concentration on Prices Paid for Cattle*.
GIPSA-RR 96-5	Marvin L. Hayenga, V.J. Rhodes, Glenn A. Grimes, and John D. Lawrence, *Vertical Coordination in Hog Production*.
GIPSA-RR 96-6	Azzeddine Azzam and Dale Anderson, *Assessing Competition in Meatpacking: Economic History, Theory, and Evidence*. This project reviewed relevant research literature.

The seventh project analyzed hog procurement in the eastern Corn Belt and was conducted by the Economic Research Service, U.S. Department of Agriculture. The findings of this project are included in the summary report on the study referenced above and are not published in a separate technical report.

This report is based on work performed under contract for GIPSA, USDA. The views expressed in this report and those of the authors and are not necessarily those of GIPSA or USDA.

VERTICAL COORDINATION IN HOG PRODUCTION

by

Marvin L. Hayenga
V.J. Rhodes
Glenn A. Grimes
John D. Lawrence

(HRGL Partnership)

4019 Stone Brooke Road
Ames, IA 50010-2900

Prepared for the
Packers and Stockyards Programs
Grain Inspection, Packers and Stockyards Administration
U.S. Department of Agriculture
Contract No. 53-6395-2-127

Table of Contents

Abstract v

Study Summary and Implications vi
    Survey Results vi
    Implications vii
    Policy or Regulatory Issues viii

Introduction 1

Literature Review 1
    Industrial Organization and Management Literature 2
    Agricultural Economics Literature 4

Study Objectives and Procedures 6

Large Pork Slaughter Firm Survey 7
    Sources of Packer Hogs -- 1993 8
    Expected Sources of Packer Hogs -- 1998 9
    Long-term Marketing Contracts 9
        Contract Provisions 9
        Long-Term Contract Advantages/Disadvantages 10
    Production Contracts/Own Production 11
    Expected Producer/Packer Linkages 12
    Packer-Hog Production Coordination Overview 13

Survey of Very Large Producers 20
    Forward Contracts and Other Pricing Methods 20
    Projections 21
    Types of Forward Contracts 21
    Advantages and Disadvantages of Forward Contracts 22
    Feed Company Relationship 23
    Contract Finishing 23
    Contract Farrowing 25
    Procurement of Breeding Stock 25
    Expected Industry Changes -- Next 5 Years 26

Large Feed Company Survey 42
    Financing Programs 42
    Advantages and Disadvantages of Financing Programs 43
    Future Direction of Financing Programs 44
    Future Direction of the Hog Industry -- Next 5 Years 44
    Benefits and Challenges to Feed Companies 45
    Hog Production by Feed Companies 45
    Summary and Overview 46

An Integrated Analysis 52
    Packer-Larger Producers Long-Term Marketing Contract Rationale 52
    Vertical Integration -- Packing and Hog Production 54
        Vertical Integration of Two Packers into Hog Production 54
        Vertical Integration of Three Large Producers into Packing 55
    Horizontal versus Vertical Contracting in the Future 57
    Structure, Conduct, and Performance of the Pork Production Sector 58
    Marketing Contracts and Vertical Integration Impacts 59

References 60

Appendix I. Survey Forms Used 62
    Survey of Pork Packers 63
    Survey of Pork Producers 69
    Survey of Large Feed Companies 87

Abstract

Vertical Coordination in Hog Production

by
Marvin L. Hayenga, V.J. Rhodes,
Glenn A. Grimes, and John D. Lawrence
(HRGL Partnership)

This study focuses on the largest packers, feed companies, and hog producers/contractors which both embody and transmit the driving forces toward change in pork sector coordination and organization linkages. The current coordination arrangements, their underlying rationale and problems, and projections of likely changes and their implications are the subjects of telephone surveys and analysis conducted by the research team. In 1993, the largest packers obtained 87 percent of their hogs through spot market arrangements, 11 percent through long-term marketing contracts and 2 percent through direct and contract production. However, long-term marketing contracts and production contracts are expected to double or triple in importance in the next 5 years. The largest hog producers accounted for much of the production contracting with other hog producers. Their sales to packers constituted most of the long-term marketing contract volume with the largest packers in 1993. A few of the largest feed companies are involved in large-scale hog production, and a few other large feed companies do some financing of feed sales. While the 1993 situation does not suggest any significant regulatory issues are imminent, if the expected rapid growth in long-term arrangements occurs in the next 5 years and continues beyond that, market access for new entrants and the reliability of spot market price information could become increasing concerns.

Study Summary and Implications

This study focuses on the largest packers, feed companies and hog producers/contractors. These participants embody and transmit the driving forces toward change in pork sector coordination and organization linkages. Telephone surveys were conducted to explore their coordination arrangements with hog producers or involvement in hog production, their underlying rationale for and problems with those arrangements, and projections of likely changes and associated implications.

Survey Results

Independent hog producers and packers linked by spot markets are still the dominant coordination method in the pork sector. The 19 large packers surveyed expect their reliance on spot markets to decline from 87 percent in 1993 to 68 percent of their hog supplies in the next 5 years. Only 13 percent of 1993 supplies were from long-term marketing contracts (11 percent), production contracts (1 percent) or production of hogs in packer-owned or joint venture facilities (1 percent). These packers expect the portion of their supply from long-term marketing contracts to reach 25 percent in 5 years, and to triple the tiny portion of their hog supply from their own production. Five of the 19 packers (but only one of the 5 largest) controlled production on some hogs through self-production or contract production.

The largest 45 hog producers (each marketing more than 60,000 head in 1993) marketed a total of 11.75 million market hogs, constituting 12.6 percent of national commercial slaughter. Because they marketed nearly 75 percent of their market hogs via long-term marketing contracts, they must have been the primary source of the marketing contract hogs obtained by these 19 packers. Large producers and long-term contracts were relatively more important in the Southeast than in the Corn Belt. These producers project rapid growth in their hog production, and their reliance on marketing contracts is consistent with packers projected increased use of long-term marketing contracts. We expect other large and intermediate-sized producers also to get more involved in such arrangements with packers, in response to increasing concern about market access among other producers and packers as these changes occur.

Contrary to public perception, a majority of contract production is done by producer-contractors rather than by packers or feed companies. Of the 45 largest producers, 39 produced some or all of their hogs via contract farrowing or, more frequently, contract finishing. For the 45 producers, 65 percent of their market hogs were contract finished and 40 percent were contract farrowed utilizing other producers' facilities and labor. The most important benefit of contract production for contractor-producers is the increased leverage of contractor's capital because land and facilities are provided by the producer-grower, leading to more rapid growth potential.

Five of the largest feed companies are involved in large-scale contract hog production. Yet, most other large feed companies have little involvement in hog production except through a modest amount of financing feed sales to hog producers directly or through their dealers. Most feed companies expected that their financing involvement would increase. The five feed companies that are involved in large-scale hog production originally began it to utilize excess feed mill capacity. The feed division and the hog production units are usually separate profit centers, and not closely linked managerially. Many packers and large producers expect a diminished role for feed companies in hog production.

The motivations for the use and expected growth of longer-term linkages between packers and producers are different for each party. The packers using marketing contracts often cited improved quality as the most important advantage. In contrast, reduced market price risk was most frequently cited as the most important advantage of forward contracts in the North Central Region (NCR) by producers. However, an assured market outlet (shackle space) was more frequently mentioned by producers in the rest of the Nation. Beginning production of many thousands of market hogs without having an assured home for them is viewed as risky, especially in areas where there are few large packers.

Nearly all of the 1.8 million hogs produced under packer control -- through contract production, joint ventures, or own production -- were produced by six large producers that were wholly or partially owned by packers. Two packer-producers were major producers before they acquired a packing plant. These two producers initiating vertical integration probably were able to reduce transaction costs and enhance their merchandising of pork through better control of quantity and quality of hog supplies. Two large producers have either opened a packing plant since the survey was conducted (Premium Standard Farms) or had one under construction in 1995 (Seaboard). Two packers initiated production because of the large profits obtainable from large- scale hog production; a secondary motive probably was also to minimize transaction costs. Case studies show that transaction cost minimization is helpful but quite incomplete in explaining the coordination changes underway in the pork sector.

Implications

In 1993, the extent of long-term producer-packer relationships or self-production by packers was too small to have major industry impacts. Yet, there are incremental changes associated with increasing long-term coordination arrangements that are beginning to emerge. A more rapid shift to producing higher-quality pork is beginning; high quality is required in many long-term coordination arrangements, and independent producers are becoming more sensitized to the need for high, consistent quality in order to be competitive. It seems likely that these arrangements have facilitated additional capital inflow into pork production, resulting in increased pork supply and/or tighter margins for hog producers. These arrangements may be essential for the entry of packers into new hog production areas such as Oklahoma and Utah and may have facilitated the expansion of packers outside the NCR.

Long-term marketing contracts with packers usually involve formula pricing with little control of production methods. Those contracts do not shift price risk to packers. A few contracts with risk sharing mechanisms do redistribute price risk between packer and producer. This practice may facilitate expanded pork production, but may also create periods (like late

1994) of lower profits for packers offering those contracts. This risk probably will limit the volume of hogs which individual packers will be willing to buy under such arrangements.

Since hog production usually is one of the better profit generators for farmers, production contracts and self-production by packers generally should be profitable, but the cyclical nature of pork production and the significant recent expansion by large producers both can contribute to periods of low or negative returns in pork production. That may result in more stable overall returns for packers involved in pork production or in risk sharing contracts, as packer margins typically improve when the production cycle peaks.

The more tightly linked pork sector will still be dominated by spot market arrangements in the next 5 years or longer, but issues may begin to arise associated with these expected changes, especially in areas outside the Corn Belt. If long-term arrangements become dominant, the probable impacts would include: (1) quicker responsiveness to consumer demands, including higher quality products; (2) possibly more branded and differentiated products; (3) more stable production levels seasonally and cyclically; (4) less spot market volume, with associated problems of more limited market access for small producers and increased short-term price volatility for their hogs; and (5) reduced transaction costs for participants in the long-term arrangements.

Policy or Regulatory Issues

Will market foreclosure become a problem? Will there be adequate access to raw materials (hogs) for packers competing with packers linked to producers with long-term arrangements? Entrants might have to develop long-term arrangements with hog producers (especially those nearing the end of a contractual arrangement) or buy from smaller producers or from producers with less desirable quality hogs who are not currently involved in long-term arrangements, or consider producing some hogs themselves.

Currently, full daily access to slaughter plants is a concern of very large producers outside of the North Central Region. This could become a more general problem if long-term arrangements became dominant, if excess capacity in hog slaughter plants no longer was prevalent most of the time, or both. Smaller producers may be more apt to be concerned, because there are natural scale economies for packers in dealing with a few large producers versus many small producers. Producer cooperatives involved in slaughter (e.g., Farmland), and cooperative or individual producer contracting arrangements with packers may be helpful if those situations occur. The access concerns of small producers may be addressed, at least to some extent, by Section 202 of the Packers and Stockyards Act, which includes clauses prohibiting unjustly discriminatory practices, or giving undue or unreasonable preference or advantage to any particular person or locality.

Using these arrangements to foreclose competitors (packers) from access to raw material supplies is the issue raised in the industrial organization literature. The extent of tying up even the best quality hogs in long-term contracts would have to be much greater before that would cause a significant anticompetitive impact in the NCR, though that could become an issue more quickly in other areas like North Carolina. Packers could remedy that by following the strategy of self-production or long-term contract arrangements. Entrants might find it more difficult to enter meat packing; they would have to enter pork production and packing at the same time, induce others to enter pork production to supply their needs, or induce producers with expiring long-term contracts to shift to them, if enough spot market supplies were not available. Such barriers to entry appear to be modest, given sufficient packers' capital, since entry into pork production is quite easy, except where corporate or packer involvement in hog production is prohibited by state law or is made difficult by organized local opposition of the not-in-my-backyard type. Those laws and attitudes could make entry by new competitors in those states much more difficult. The share of hog production and processing in those states may suffer if prohibited ownership or contract links are the preferred coordination system, and the costs associated with second-best arrangements exceed the other benefits associated with locating in those states.

Will a shift to more long-term coordination arrangements increase packer concentration and market power? As noted above, they may make entry more difficult, and possibly more capital intensive, by requiring the development of hog supplies in some way jointly with building the packing plant and developing product merchandising arrangements. Reliance upon spot market competition for a major part of hog supplies would become increasingly difficult. Yet, the current development of plants in fringe production areas may have been impractical without such long-term arrangements and/or self-production. In such cases, they may contribute to increased industry production, competition in product markets (and possibly hog procurement if they partially use independent producer supply), and shifts in the location of hog production.

Long-term arrangements which enhance product quality may allow differentiated, and possibly branded, products to be more successfully developed. Differentiated products may allow some limited exercise of market power and enhance profitability. But higher prices for higher quality may be justifiable, and entry is unlikely to be restricted effectively. Product differentiation also might offer market niches for new entrants to exploit.

Large producers and packers expect increased concentration of volume in the hands of fewer packers and producers in the future. These expectations may be extrapolations of recent trends. If changing coordination systems lead to increased capital requirements and more complex managerial skills for entry, they could contribute to increasing concentration. Since two of the three[1] most recent entrants into meat packing have entered both hog production and meat packing, integrated or paired entry may not be that difficult.

---

[1] The three entrants were PSF, Seaboard, and Indiana Packing. Tyson, a fourth recent entrant into packing, already was a mega producer.

What are the implications for spot markets? Terminal and auction markets for market hogs, dealers, and order buyers would decline rapidly in volume, following current trends. Spot markets for the residual supply and demand would become more thinly traded, and probably more volatile as the "shock absorber" for unanticipated changes in supply and demand. Price reporting would become more difficult, and concern about price manipulation would escalate as relatively small changes in the behavior of large market participants more likely could have an impact on reported market prices. Some formula pricing arrangements based on declining volume markets would have to be renegotiated. The ongoing restructuring of the Chicago Mercantile Exchange live hog futures contract (formerly based on delivery to several terminal markets) is a consequence of these changes. Government agencies will have to consider whether reporting contract terms in a market for differentiated contracts would be feasible and a contribution to improved or more equitable market performance, enough to justify using public funds for the service.

Overall, the 1993 situation does not suggest any significant regulatory issues are imminent. However, if the expected rapid growth in long-term arrangements occurs in the next 5 years, and continues beyond that, regulatory agencies may have to periodically track changes in coordination systems and more closely monitor pork sector behavior.

Introduction

This study of vertical coordination in the pork sector was initiated by the USDA's Packers and Stockyards Administration now Packers and Stockyards Programs, Grain Inspection, Packers and Stockyards Administration (GIPSA) in response to a Congressionally mandated study of concentration of the red meat packing industry. With assistance from an interagency task force, GIPSA requested proposals for analysis of the economics of vertical integration and coordination arrangements in the hog-pork sector, and the implications of those linkages for future structure, conduct, and performance in the hog slaughtering and processing industry. GIPSA indicated an interest in the extent of use of various vertical coordination arrangements, their terms, reasons for their use, likely future directions of change in coordination arrangements, and their implications for hog producers and slaughterers. Who will control agricultural production is often a policy issue at the national, state, and local levels of government. Long-term production and marketing contracts or vertical integration into hog production by packers, feed companies, or other large-scale hog producers may have both policy and regulatory implications. Consequently, an analysis focusing on long-term coordination methods, and their perceived advantages and disadvantages relative to the spot market, may provide insight into the likely evolution of pork sector coordination systems, and corresponding implications for pork sector participants, policy makers, and regulatory agencies.

This study focuses on the largest packers, feed companies and hog producers/contractors which both embody and transmit the driving forces toward change in pork sector coordination and organization linkages. The current coordination arrangements with hog producers (and each other), their underlying rationale and problems, projections of likely changes and their implications are the subjects of surveys conducted by the research team. In addition, the research team summarizes prior research and offers an appraisal of ongoing changes in sector coordination and their performance implications.

The report begins with a brief review of previous research. The results of the largest meat packer, feed company, and hog producer/integrator surveys are presented. An evaluation of the collective results of the surveys and other relevant factors influencing coordination system and sector performance changes follows.

Literature Review

When might the vertical series of activities involved in producing a consumer good be conducted by a series of independent firms interacting freely in markets, by firms interacting less freely through a set of marketing and production contractual linkages, or by a single vertically-integrated firm? The relevant literature includes the evolving contributions of industrial organization economists and strategic management experts on the motivations for vertical integration or contractual linkages, and applied research on changing vertical linkages in the pork sector and the broiler sector (often considered the industrialized analog and, perhaps, forerunner of developments in the pork sector).

Industrial Organization and Management Literature

In the industrial organization literature, *The Handbook of Industrial Organization* (Vol. 1, 1989) summarizes most of the motivations for tighter vertical integration or contractual coordination linkages in three review papers by Oliver Williamson (transaction costs), Martin Perry (market power), and Michael Katz (contractual incentives). From the strategic management perspective, J. T. Mahoney suggests other factors influencing the difficulty of establishing an equitable contract and monitoring the results, and the corresponding likelihood of vertical integration.

O. E. Williamson has developed the most generally accepted thesis that the vertical coordination method which minimizes transaction costs will prevail. Williamson's various studies in the past 30 years were further developments of a classic study in 1937 by Ronald Coase on the nature of the firm. Williamson has argued for crucial roles of enterprise-specific assets, and uncertainty and constrained information in determining the degree of vertical integration. Any producer with considerable investments which have little value except in a highly specific use such as sow farrowing or broiler slaughter must take measures to protect against opportunistic behavior by the other side of the market, especially when there is not active competition on that side. Thus, Williamson has argued that the investments in facilities and equipment which are not multipurpose, and in situations where reliance on the market is judged too risky, will lead to contractual or ownership vertical integration.

Perry has argued that the broad determinants of vertical integration are technological economies (a more efficient production frontier using primary instead of intermediate inputs, e.g., feed instead of the pig), transaction economies (advantages using primary rather than intermediate markets), and market imperfections. If a stage of the market system has market power, then lower production levels, higher prices, and less efficient resource allocation are likely results. An integrator may reduce those inefficiencies by internalizing those production and price decisions, and possibly extract more profits from the competitive stage, while making it more difficult for current or potential competitors to expand or enter, respectively. In addition, vertical integration may diversify risk (if profits at adjacent stages are negatively correlated), assure supplies or markets, allow for the acquisition of useful information to monitor others dealing with them, synchronize input and product flows, and capture economies of scope (e.g., spreading market research costs over two enterprises) or scale.

Market foreclosure of competitors' access to input or product markets is often cited as a possible adverse effect of vertical integration. Perry suggests that the integrated firm has to have a substantial market share before foreclosure can be effective and few gains in efficiency to balance the undesirable effects from foreclosure before it would be viewed as an overall negative influence on industry/market performance.

In addition, Perry suggests that the first firms to link up vertically reduce the number of alternative sources (outlets) for others, thus thinning the market. A thin market can increase the costs of market or contractual exchange for others, and stimulate subsequent integration by others.

Katz suggests that products in intermediate markets may possess very complex bundles of attributes, making problems of opportunistic behavior by contract participants more severe, or at least more complicated. Purchase/sales contracts at one stage may affect the equilibrium of the downstage product market competitive game. Contract provisions such as volume discount pricing, tying arrangements (you can buy A only if you also buy B), and restricted or exclusive dealing arrangements are sometimes viewed as forms of vertical restraint. Sophisticated pricing arrangements and vertical restraints are responses to the problems of opportunistic behavior by market suppliers or customers and the need to share risk. If neither party at the time of contracting knows the value of the product, or there is unequal information available to contracting parties, risk aversion may lead to risk sharing. If product reputation might be adversely impacted through improper behavior of a supplier or customer, tighter vertical linkages may be necessary.

Payment schemes based on relative performance may provide insurance and incentives to contracting parties when they have incomplete information regarding performance or difficulty in monitoring behavior under the contract. These can increase contractor profits in some environments.

If vertical linkages lead to reduced consumer search costs or lower cross elasticities of demand through increased product differentiation, higher industry profits could result. While vertical restraints may restrict entry, they may also enhance entry if increased product differentiation makes it easier for a new entrant to find a profitable market niche.

After review of the literature on vertical restraints, Katz concludes that there is no widespread agreement whether a particular practice is socially beneficial or harmful. All of the practices can be beneficial in some instances and harmful in others, and it may be extremely difficult to distinguish between the two cases. Most courts and economists have focused on the degree of market concentration in the belief that vertical agreements are unlikely to have anti-competitive effects when they involve parties with low market shares in upstream and downstream markets. Katz argues that the analysis needs to be expanded to consider the markets' information structure, risk characteristics (size of sunk investment), the degree to which parties become locked in to one another (the amount of transaction-specific capital), and the opportunity costs associated with different institutional and contractual linkages that are potential substitutes.

According to Mahoney, if the task is easy to understand and monitor, then it is easier to establish contract terms and monitor the results. If it is difficult to ascertain and reward individual effort, then establishing equitable contract terms is more difficult, and integration is more likely.

Agricultural Economics Literature

Mighell and Jones published the seminal work on vertical coordination in agriculture in 1963. This classic study estimated the volume marketed via various coordination methods at the first handler level in all major agricultural commodities. They emphasized the differences between marketing contracts and various forms of contract production typified by a contractor providing various resources (e.g., chicks, feed, managerial oversight) to a grower providing facilities and daily care. Goldberg provided a more in-depth analysis of the coordination system in three vertical commodity systems in 1968. The regional research group, NC-117, published a summary of their efforts to understand and document vertical coordination systems in eight commodity sectors, including pork, in a book edited by Bruce Marion in 1986. Barry et al., reviewed the theoretical developments influencing the nature of firm and industry coordination, noting especially the risk reduction and increasing capital availability incentives for contracting, especially in the 1980s in agriculture.

L. Martin et al., at the George Morris Centre, reviewed the vertical coordination literature as part of a five-country comparison of broiler industry coordination systems. They distinguished equity partnerships (involving some transfer of assets) and nonequity partnerships (four forms are typical: service contracts, supply contracts, distribution contracts, and marketing contracts). They concluded "that the organizational form (structure) of the vertical relationship depends on the nature of:

1. the tasks performed by each party,
2. specific human and physical assets used in production/marketing,
3. how well performance can be measured,
4. the absence or existence of trust between parties, and
5. the risks involved in the production process and in the relationship."

They argued that a variety of conditions in an industry could logically result in a variety of governance structures existing in that industry.

Sauvee thoroughly surveyed the vertical coordination literature in 1994. He attempted to show the relationships among the evolving theoretical developments, and tried to integrate them using the U.S. broiler industry as a case study. He concluded that he was unable to satisfactorily explain why heterogenous vertical business linkages emerge, remain, and compete. That remains as a challenge for future research.

In the 1950s and 1960s, the broiler industry began to adopt new technologies, increased size and sophistication of production units, and embarked on an economic restructuring that has been characterized as the prototype of the industrialization of agriculture. Various pork industry participants, including feed companies and meat packers, began to experiment with production contracts and concerns began to be raised during the late 1960s whether the pork industry was going to emulate the broiler industry. Generally the feed company and pork packer trials of production contracts were unprofitable and largely subsided in the 1970s.

In the 1960s, the economies of specialization and scale in cattle feeding and the increased feed grain supply in the High Plains led to the rapid industrialization of that phase of the cattle industry. Although some economists, on the basis of a vaguely understood broiler model, projected extensive vertical integration of beef packing and cattle feeding, such integration has been minor.

Hog production in the past quarter century has become industrialized in the sense that most hogs are now produced in factory-like confinement, and approximately half are tended by people who are often entirely specialized into hog production or even into specialized tasks such as farrowing. Whereas 100 sows was a large unit 25 years ago, 500 to 3,500 sow units are now being built, and the leading producers now own and control many units of that size. Rhodes and Grimes have documented this transformation of hog production and the coordination systems employed in nine periodic national surveys of hog producers over 20 years (1974-1994).

Contract production of hogs is considered by most observers to be vertical coordination. That is correct when feed companies or packers engage in contract production. However, a majority of contract hog production is horizontal contracting among producers. A producer with more assets, management skills, and/or a willingness to take risks provides the hogs (breeding stock or pigs) and the feed to another producer who raises them. The producer/grower has incentives that generally arise from a lack of capital, management skills, or willingness to take large risks. This significant and growing share of contract hog production, which interests -- and even disturbs -- many farmers, needs to be distinguished from other contract production that involves vertical coordination. The incentive structures for the two types of contract production differ although they overlap.

Various studies have looked at the extent and type of vertical coordination in the hog industry. Hayenga et al., 1972, reported on an important survey on vertical coordination in the pork industry in 1972. Hayenga et al., 1985, summarized many subsequent studies. They conclude that (1) vertical integration in the pork industry was relatively uncommon, (2) production contracts had gone nowhere in the Midwest, but had received greater use in the Southeast, and (3) the noncontractual marketing system was offering adequate supplies and market outlets, resulting in insufficient incentives for the pork industry to become highly integrated by ownership or contract as in the broiler industry. However, a 1992 Hayenga and Kimle survey of the 22 largest packers led to a different conclusion -- that packers' production and marketing contracts with hog producers would expand dramatically in the next decade, triggered more by quality concerns than supply uncertainty. Azzam and Wellman, 1992, published an estimate that 8 percent of the largest packers' hog suppliers were owned or contracted.

The broiler industry experience also may offer insights into likely developments or issues emerging in the pork sector, especially since some of the largest operations were begun by broiler industry participants. The development of "integrators" like Tyson Foods that own and/or direct the entire productive process from the production of hatching eggs through the merchandising of ready-to-eat sized broiler portions to the nation's restaurants was an advance in organizational efficiency. Production contracts have been integral elements in the growth of such integrators. Vertical integration and the production contract for broilers so captured agriculture's attention that, perhaps, too little attention was given to the tremendous changes in scale and the success of the integrators in capturing a whole series of innovation-related profits associated with technical and organizational gains in lowering the costs of production.

The broiler industry has specific assets at several levels (breeding flocks, hatcheries, broiler houses, and processing plants), a short biological process, and a perishable product. These factors have led to a tightly coordinated flow of eggs, chicks and broilers to minimize transaction costs and risks, and achieve the low production costs associated with full utilization of all investments and committed labor and management. So the integrator in broilers superseded the market.

The bulk of the industrialization of broilers occurred in the single decade of the 1950s, although the concentration of integrators continues. The lessons also were applied to turkeys. While turkey production is now dominated by integrators and most production has been moved from seasonal, open-range to year-round confinement buildings, its industrialization moved much more slowly and less completely than the broiler sector. The evolution of these industries may offer some insights into ongoing changes in the pork industry. The differing evolutionary paths of broilers, turkeys, and cattle feeding warn against use of any one of them as a road map for hogs.

Study Objectives and Procedures

The studies cited have documented the coordination system changes occurring in the pork industry and some possible reasons for them. However, recent changes in long-term arrangements between hog producers, meat packers, and other industry participants have not been comprehensively documented and analyzed. Innovative linkages among hog producers, integrators, contractors, feed suppliers, breeding stock suppliers and/or meat packers are emerging. Of particular interest are several vertical coordination initiatives by meat packers into hog production via ownership, joint venture, or production contracts. Further, there are long-term marketing contracts between meat packers and hog producers which are relatively new initiatives growing in importance, sometimes linked to approved or packer-supplied breeding stock. Will these grow and effect significant change in industry competitive structure and performance? The current and likely use of the arrangements noted above needs to be estimated to better assess whether they are likely to affect competition and pork sector performance.

The objectives of this study are to:

1. determine the relative importance of each type of vertical coordination arrangement;

2. document the types and provisions of these ownership or long-term contract arrangements;
3. determine motivations and incentives for these vertical arrangements;
4. analyze the interrelationship among the vertical arrangements and packing industry structure, conduct and performance; and
5. assess likely future levels and location of vertical coordination relationships, and their implications.

This study focuses on the firms expected to be the most significant innovators in offering new vertical coordination arrangements in the pork industry. Telephone survey instruments were developed for the largest pork packers, the largest hog producers/contractors, and the largest feed companies.[2] Three survey instruments were developed together to provide appropriate consistency among topics and the form with the questions posed in the surveys (Appendix). The surveys were reviewed by GIPSA for consistency with Office of Management and Budget requirements and were approved by the Office of Management and Budget. Descriptive statistics are provided on the degree to which long-term coordination arrangements are used, the rationale for their use, the projections of likely use in years, and their projections of industry trends and their implications. Since the three surveys are not representative samples of their respective segments of the pork sector, statistical tests are not appropriate.

These surveys were answered on a voluntary basis by busy executives with less than perfect information about the industry and probably with fuzzy visions of future events. We believe that their answers help to describe and analyze the industry but there is no claim to perfect accuracy or foresight.

Large Pork Slaughter Firm Survey

A telephone survey of the 20 largest pork slaughter firms (Table 1) was conducted in late January and February 1994. The list of the largest pork slaughter firms was available from prior Iowa State University packer surveys (Hayenga, 1994). Survey respondents were usually the managers of hog procurement operations or other senior managers very familiar with hog procurement operations and strategy. The survey focused on: (1) their coordination linkages with hog production operations in calendar year 1993; (2) expected changes in the hog procurement arrangements in their company over the next 5 years; (3) advantages and disadvantages of their production contracts or longer term (longer than 6 months) marketing contracts with hog producers; and (4) their joint venture or solely owned hog production

---

[2]The largest 20 pork slaughter firms (those with plants exceeding 4,000 head daily slaughter capacity) accounted for 90 percent of federally inspected slaughter, and the largest 45 hog producers accounted for 13 percent of hog production in 1993. The largest feed manufacturers surveyed includes all those with any significant volume of feed sold to hog producers.

operations. In addition, the packer managers were asked what changes they expected in linkages between packers and hog producers and the problems or benefits expected from those changes. Only one packer, operating a single plant, elected not to respond to the survey. Since this was not a representative sample of all packers, the data reported below should not be generalized beyond the surveyed group of packers representing 86.5 percent of federally inspected commercial slaughter in 1993.

Sources of Packer Hogs -- 1993

The 19 pork slaughter firm respondents slaughtered 78.6 million hogs in 1993 (Table 2). Approximately 87 percent of the hogs slaughtered by these packers were spot market purchases: 68 percent were from deliveries to their packing plant or buying station; approximately 2 percent were acquired at terminal or auction markets; and 16 percent were purchased through dealers or order buyers (sometimes exclusively for a single packer).

The very low volume currently coming from terminals and auction markets is a dramatic change from the marketing system of 60 years ago when those were the dominant methods of livestock marketing. The direct movement of hogs from increasingly large volume producers to packers now located in primary hog production areas is clearly dominant. Somewhat surprising is the reliance of a large number of packers on dealers or order buyers to supply their marginal needs. In a few cases, dealers or order buyers were exclusive suppliers to individual packers; their purchases might be considered almost in the same class as direct purchases by a packer employee.

The remainder of these packers' hog supply (13 percent) was from longer term contractual arrangements with producers or self-supply by packers; approximately 11 percent of the hogs supplied were by long-term marketing contracts (longer than 6 months)[3] involving 13 of the 19 packers responding to the survey. The remainder of packers' hog supply came from production in their own or jointly owned facilities (slightly more than 1 percent), or from contract producers' facilities (almost 1 percent). With one exception, packers involved in large-scale hog production typically had independent producers supply a high proportion of the slaughter supply to their plants in 1993.

Although the packers participating in this survey accounted for 78.6 million hogs of the 90.9 million hogs slaughtered in 1993, the relative volume acquired by various hog procurement methods employed by smaller packers may differ significantly from the behavior reported here. Thus, the percentages reported here should not be generalized to the entire industry. However, if no long-term arrangements or self-production were used by smaller packers and the large packer

---

[3]This includes the "other" classification in the table, which also could be classified as a long-term marketing contract.

not participating in this survey, 11 percent of the nation's hogs would be involved in those type of arrangements in 1993.

Expected Sources of Packer Hogs -- 1998

Each packer was asked how their hog supply arrangements were expected to change 5 years in the future. The changes which they collectively expected in their operations is dramatic.[4]

The percentage of purchases from the spot market by these packers is expected to drop by 24 percent (from 87 percent to 66 percent), with half of that decline from reduced order buyer or dealer volume. The decline in expected spot market purchases at plant or buying stations accounts for the other half of the expected decline in spot market purchases.

Long-term marketing contracts are expected to grow sharply in volume, increasing from 11 percent in 1993 to over 25 percent in 5 years. Packers' controlled production of market hogs is expected to triple, growing from more than 2 percent (split between own or contract production) to 7 percent; most of the expected increase is in their own or joint venture production facilities, though production contract volume is also expected to increase.

Long-term Marketing Contracts

Based on recent surveys (Hayenga and Kimle, 1992) and reports in trade publications, large packers were expected to be more innovative than smaller packers in changing coordination arrangements. Most large packers are now involved in long-term contracts on at least an experimental or pilot project basis, or are considering such arrangements as part of their long-term procurement strategy.

Contract Provisions. Although some long-term marketing contracts with hog producers were described as continuing, sometimes on a hand-shake basis, more than half of the hogs acquired under long-term contracts were via formal, written contracts with a definite term (often ranging from 4 to 7 years).[5] Approximately half of the packers involved in these arrangements reported requiring a minimum volume to be supplied, and either the minimum quality of hog to

---

[4]Individual responses were weighted by 1993 slaughter volumes to provide an estimate of the aggregate change from the firms interviewed.

[5]Some packers had shorter term fixed price forward marketing contracts of a few months in duration, ranging up to 6 months in length for specific groups of hogs, usually based upon the Chicago Mercantile Exchange live hog futures contract. This volume was quite small and was included in spot market volumes.

be supplied or their breeding or genetics (Table 3). The feed or nutrition program and approval of facilities were part of the contract for a few packers. Other contractual requirements were each mentioned by only one respondent; herd health or drug withdrawal programs and year-round or exclusive supply arrangements were two areas of contract provisions worth noting.

The dominant pricing arrangement was a formula price plus a carcass merit adjustment based upon cutout value of the hogs delivered. The base price typically is based upon some specified single (or an average of several) current market price reports (usually USDA) considered representative by both parties to the contract; sometimes these are based upon markets which are some distance from the local market (perhaps to minimize concerns about local market price representativeness). A few contracts involve some innovative attempts to limit or share risks, such as tying prices to hog production costs by incorporating feed grain or soybean meal prices in a formula priced contract, or providing upper and lower bounds on prices paid over the length of the contract, or sharing the pain or gain from extremely high or low prices outside of established price boundaries.

Packers typically provided an assured market outlet with a known pricing arrangement, but little else to their contract suppliers. Two packers reported offering credit or loan assistance, and one respondent reported providing breeding stock. Providing detailed carcass cutout data was mentioned by one respondent; that practice is becoming more common in the packing industry.

Long-term Contract Advantages/Disadvantages. Packers were asked what they considered the primary reasons for using long-term contracts, the primary disadvantages, as well as their perceptions about the primary advantages and disadvantages of these arrangements for their contract partners -- the hog producers[6] (tables 4 and 5).

Improving the quality of hogs acquired, increasing consistency of supply, and increasing the volume of hogs supplied to their plants were the most frequently mentioned reasons for using long-term contracts, with no appreciable differences between Midwest and other packers. Of these, improved quality or reduced quality risk stood out as the most important reasons, ranked first or second by 7 of the 10 firms responding to this question. Consistent supplies was mentioned by five respondents, with 3 ranking it most important. Only 2 of the 10 firms responding did not mention at least one of these three reasons for using long-term marketing contracts. A few packers noted that they were responding to rivals or to the current or perceived future demands of large hog producers for these types of programs. Although plant efficiency, improved scheduling, reduced transaction costs, or increased profits were not mentioned as important advantages to contracts by packers, most of the mentioned advantages contribute to improved profits.

---

[6]Except for three packers who required examination of the survey form before they would participate in the survey, all responses were unprompted responses to a telephone survey.

The number of long-term contract disadvantages cited by packers were fewer than the perceived advantages cited by those packers with experience with long-term marketing contracts. Four packers mentioned that they bore more price risk, and three acknowledged some type of reduced flexibility due to the long-term nature of their contracts. Only one packer felt higher prices were being paid for hogs under contract terms.

Packers with long-term marketing contracts were asked their perceptions of the advantages and disadvantages of those contracts for the hog producers involved in those contracts (table 5). They perceived more advantages than disadvantages. Financial advantages were rated the primary benefit to pork producers with long-term marketing contracts. In some cases, increased capital availability was listed as most important; in others it was lower financial risk. Financial benefits were ranked first, second, or both by half of the packers responding to this question. The other response rated first by several packers was assured access to markets, with approximately one-third of packer respondents mentioning that as a benefit. A wide variety of perceived benefits were mentioned only once, e.g., no hassle or no worries regarding marketing, lower transaction cost, assured price, quality premiums, and complete cutout data.

The most frequent disadvantage perceived by packers for pork producers was the reduced flexibility allowed under the contract. A couple of packers also noted the limitation on the producers' ability to shop around for a better price when contract prices sometimes would not be as high as spot market prices.

Production Contracts/Own Production

Only four packers reported any appreciable volume of hog production in their own, joint venture, or production contract facilities. Improved control of quality and volume and increased volume were the most frequently noted reasons for their own hog production. Increased profits or, in the case of a joint venture, reduced risk were offered usually as less important, but contributing factors by a few respondents.

The primary perceived benefits for contract producers (growers) or joint venture partners mentioned most often by packers were assured market access and improved financial leverage, capital availability, or reduced risk. Better facility and labor utilization were also mentioned by two respondents.

The most important perceived disadvantages for contract producers or joint venture partners were reduced independence and flexibility. One packer noted the limited time left on a particular contract as a disadvantage for the contract producer.

Packers were asked what the net benefits of long-term contract or self-production arrangements were for their operations. Most packers could not provide quantitative estimates of the net benefits of long-term marketing contracts. A few respondents felt there were no net benefits compared to spot market arrangements -- that it was a break-even proposition. A few others provided estimates that were quite small (from near zero to a high of 2.3 cents per pound of carcass). Only three respondents estimated benefits of production contracts, joint venture, or production of hogs in their own facilities. Estimated benefits ranged from zero to $20 per head; the highest estimate was purely a forecast and was not based on actual results.

Estimating net benefits from production or long-term marketing arrangements is difficult, and only a small number of those packers participating in such arrangements offered estimates. Hog production profits are highly cyclical, and packers with limited experience may have experienced the very good, the very poor, or all profit portions of the production cycle. Consequently, a wide range of estimates should have been expected. The long-term marketing contract arrangements involve a larger number of packers and most arrangements are tied to reported spot market prices. Thus, it is not surprising to find little estimated price benefit. Two respondents said there was no net benefit, at least in the short run. One or more respondent(s) noted benefits from lower procurement transaction costs, quality improvements, or transport efficiencies. Since these packer respondents were usually operating in different profit centers than those in actual hog production in their firms, they were not necessarily aware of the profits being made in hog production.

Expected Producer/Packer Linkages

The largest packers were asked what general changes they expected in the linkages among packers and hog producers and hog production in the next 5 years. The response received from most survey respondents was closer producer-packer relationships, expressed in a number of ways. These included longer term relationships like marketing contracts, or continuing, perhaps more informal, supplier-packer relationships based on the quality of hogs produced or the herd health programs utilized for packer acceptance. The descriptive terms used included continuing or closer relationships or linkages, quality partnerships, guaranteed access agreements, and voluntary integration.

Packers expect that the need for consistent supply and quality will be met by a variety of voluntary arrangements with pork producers, with packers playing a greater role in controlling their raw material supply, or by packers getting more involved in hog production themselves. More packer feeding, integration by ownership or contract, or establishing a portion of slaughter needs in advance were expected by several packers. With more direct linkages between packers and hog producers, terminal markets were not expected to survive, according to a couple of packers.

Several packers forecast continued growth in the size of pork producers, smaller producers dropping out, and packers less inclined to deal with small producers. Value-based pricing was expected to become more prevalent and greater emphasis on meat quality was expected by a small number of packers.

The most frequently mentioned expected benefit of likely changes in producer/packer linkages was improved control of product quality. More than half of the respondents noted quality in some way. This not only involves leanness, which many people would consider the primary quality attribute for pork; quality of the lean; consistency of size and quality of the consumer product; and the ability to market certified residue-free product were mentioned. A stronger consumer orientation was expected, and increased payments based on value were expected by some respondents.

A few packers expected that the pork production and marketing system would be lower cost with tighter margins, so less efficient packers and producers would have difficulty surviving. Hog producers would be driven to higher volume production. A smaller number of packers are expected to be left in a more consolidated, less competitive packing industry, and they will be dependent on a smaller number of large pork producers. More alliances between packers and producers should lead to less reliance on daily buying, as packers would have a buffer stock. Some packers expect more difficulty in relying upon reported market prices for some pricing arrangements, and more risks to those packers involved more heavily in longer term pricing arrangements. As more self-production or contract production of hogs by packers occurs, some packers expect the location of hog production to shift as the entire system's structure changes, partly in response to restrictive legislation in some states.

Packer-Hog Production Coordination Overview

Nineteen large hog slaughter companies accounting for 86.5 percent of 1993 hog slaughter responded to a telephone survey regarding current and expected coordination arrangements used to supply their slaughter hogs. Spot market purchases of hogs dominated in 1993, accounting for 87 percent of these packers' hog supply. Only 13 percent of 1993 supplies were from long-term marketing contracts (11 percent), production contracts (1 percent) or production in packer-owned facilities (1 percent). However, the marketing contract volume has been growing in recent years.

In the next 5 years, the responding packers expect to sharply reduce their reliance on spot market purchases (from 87 to 66 percent). Half of that decline is expected from less order buyer or dealer volume, and half from reduced spot market purchases from producers. The larger packers responding to this survey expect the portion of their supply from long-term marketing contracts to reach 25 percent in 5 years, and to triple the small proportion of their hog supply from their own production, joint ventures, and production contracts.

Improved quality appears to be a primary driving force to greater reliance on long-term supply arrangements involving more packer control over what will be delivered to their loading docks, but increased volume and improved consistency (quality and quantity) of supply are overlapping reasons for the significant changes expected in their own operations and in the industry generally by the hog procurement or general managers of the large packers responding to this survey.

Increasing hog supply for their plants, especially in fringe production areas, is clearly a driving force in an industry with excess slaughter capacity where there is a strong economic incentive to keep one or two shifts of workers fully employed year-round. More consistent supplies in an industry characterized by cyclical and seasonal production of hogs also can be well understood as a factor contributing to change.

There are a few recent and emerging changes which may be stimulating further change in the pork sector. The increasing export demand for chilled pork to Japan, with its stringent quality requirements, and the likelihood of increasing trade as trade barriers decline may make it difficult for packers to merely rely upon selection from the current hog population to fill increased volume contracts. Tighter specifications on incoming raw material (hogs) may be necessary to meet tighter customer specifications and food safety. More consistent, higher-yielding carcasses should improve labor efficiency and reduce production of lower value products (e.g., lard) in slaughter/processing operations. More information regarding carcass quality provided to the packer should occur under most coordination systems, though the incentives for change appear stronger in contractually linked or integrated operations. Quality rewards in pricing systems are expected to be more prevalent in all coordination systems, though more tightly linked operations appear more likely to respond quickly to increasing quality demands by packers.

In summary, packers expect to be more involved in making or heavily influencing hog production and marketing decisions in the next 5 years. Projected changes heavily favor more long-term marketing contracts. In the fringe areas of hog production, expansion of vertical integration or joint ventures is planned for several plants. However, we should caution that the pace of change in coordination arrangements in this industry has usually been slower than forecasted. While the expected pace of change in the next 5 years is dramatic, the changes forecasted by the most well informed industry participants and analysts may be prone to error.

Table 1. Packers Interviewed -- January 1994

Name
Claugherty Packing
Dakota Pork Industries
Excel Corp.
Farmland Foods
Fisher Packing Company
Hatfields Quality Meats
George Hormel & Company
IBP
Indiana Packers Corp.
Iowa Packing Company
Sara Lee
Lykes Bros., Inc.
Monfort, Inc.
John Morrell & Company
Seaboard Farms, Pork Division
Smithfield Foods
Thorn Apple Valley
Tyson Foods
Worthington Packing Company

Table 2. Packer Coordination Arrangements,
1993 and 1998 Forecast

	1993 Volume (million hd)	1993 Volume (percent)	Expected 1998 Volume* (percent)
Spot at plant or station	53.3	67.8	58.9
Spot from terminal or auction	1.9	2.4	1.2
Spot from dealer or buyer	12.9	16.5	6.1
All spot market		68.1	86.6	66.1
Contract, continuing	3.0	3.8	11.2
Contract, def length	5.4	6.9	14.4
All market contracts		8.4	10.6	25.6
Own or joint facilities	1.1	1.4	5.1
Production contract	0.7	0.9	1.6
All own/contract production		1.8	2.3	6.7
Other		0.3	0.4	1.6
TOTAL	**78.6**	**100**	**100**

*Based on respondents' expected percentages for 1998 and weighted by respondents' 1993 volume. Some totals are affected by rounding.

Table 3. Provisions of Marketing Contracts with Producers

	Number of Responses	Simple Rank
Packer requires/producer provides		
Time length of arrangement	8	1
Min volume	7	2
Min quality	7	2
Breeding type source	6	4
Feed use type/source	3	5
Scheduled delivery times	2	7
Type of facility	3	5
Carcass size specifications	1	8
Hog health requirements	1	8
Year-round contract	1	8
Proper drug withdrawal	1	8
Continuous volume	1	8
Exclusive supply arrangement	1	8
Resources provided by packer		
Breeding stock	1	2
Credit/loan assistance	2	1
Detailed kill schedules	1	2
Other	1	2
Pricing arrangement		
Formula price	10	1
Other	1	2

Table 4. Reasons/Disadvantages for Marketing Contracts
(Reported by Packers)

	Number of Responses	Number of Rankings		
		1's[*]	2's	3's
Reasons for use				
Improved quality	5	3	2	
Consistent supplies	5	3	1	1
Increased volume	4		3	1
Less quality risk	2	2		
Rivals use it/keep up	1			1
Improved plant efficiency	1		1	
Advantageous price	1		1	
Will have to use in future	1		1	
Lower volume risk	1	1		
Reduced price risk	1	1		
Eliminate negative returns	1	1		
Necessary to serve large producer	1	1		
Disadvantages				
Higher price risk	4	4		
Reduced flexibility	2		2	
Perception that formula prices create lower market prices	1		1	
Higher prices paid	1	1		
Producers sometimes don't meet commitment	1	1		
Can't adjust kills easily	1	1		
Too dependent on few suppliers	1	1		

[*]Number one rankings reflect multiple responses by one respondent.

Table 5. Benefits/Disadvantages for Marketing Contracts for Hog Producers
(As Perceived by Packers)

	Number of Responses	Number of Rankings		
		1's	2's	3's
Benefits				
Lower financial risk	5	2	3	
Increased capital available	5	3	1	1
Assured access to market outlets	5	3		2
Higher price	1	1		
Paid premium for quality	1	1		
Assured good price	1	1		
Reduced price risk	1		1	
No worries about marketing	1		1	
No hassle each time	1		1	
Lower transaction costs	1				1
Get complete data on hogs marketed	1			1
Disadvantages				
Reduced flexibility	4	4		
Lower profits	1	1		
Lower price received when market price above contract limits	1	1		
Lower profit opportunity with lower risk contract	1	1		
Others may pay more sometimes	1	1		
Obligation to fulfill contract requirements	1		1	

Survey of Very Large Producers

Grimes and Rhodes (1994) provided a list of the nation's 65 largest hog producers, each marketing 40,000 head or more in 1993. Top executives of the 45 operations (each marketed more than 62,000 hogs and pigs in 1993) expected to be largest in 1994 were interviewed by telephone. These 45 very large producers reported marketing 13 million head of hogs and pigs in 1993, an average of 261,725 head (ranging from approximately 62,000 to more than 1.5 million head). These 45 producers are the leading edge of industry change and are treated as a population; thus, they are not viewed as representative of the entire population of producers (table 6). Evidence from this survey and the packer survey shows that the bulk of the activity involving vertical coordination and contracting occurs in this group.

The majority of these 45 operations specialize in market hog production. However, 19 are also involved in or owned by: pork slaughter/processing or joint ventures with packers; companies, individuals, or farm cooperatives involved in manufacturing or selling feed; breeding stock companies; turkey or broiler production; cattle feeding; and hog facility construction, among others.

These 13 million hogs and pigs were marketed in 22 states; about 40 percent were marketed in 10 states of the North Central Region (NCR). Leading states in the NCR were Iowa (17.1 percent of the national marketings of the group), Minnesota (7.4 percent) and Missouri (7.2 percent). The remaining 60 percent were marketed in the rest of the nation (RON), of which 49.7 percent were in North Carolina and Virginia. Note that these data indicate the location of marketing rather than of production.

Most of these producers are in an aggressive growth mode. When they were asked to project their market volume in 1998, the 41 respondents projected a total of 29.6 million hogs/pigs, an increase of 144 percent over their 1993 volume. The five major feed companies producing hogs projected an increase of 133 percent.

Forward Contracts and Other Pricing Methods

Of these 45 large producers, 27 marketed 8.7 million head (74.2 percent of the total 11 million) market hogs (MH) through forward contracts. Of these 27 producers, 22 marketed all of their slaughter hogs via marketing contracts. A few of the 7 mega producers (each marketing more than 500,000 head in 1993) forward contracted all or most of their volume. Sixteen of these 45 producers marketed 100 percent through conventional spot markets and 6 more marketed partly in that fashion for a total of 18.1 percent of the group's 11¾ million market hogs.

The other 8 percent of market volume was packer controlled via ownership, joint ventures, or contract production. Six production units were either wholly or substantially owned by companies that were packers or substantially owned by packers.[7] A few of the packer-owned producers marketed some of their hogs to other packers -- via forward contracts.

The 870,000 head listed under packer ownership, joint venture, or production contract was 7.7 percent of the group's total market hog marketings in 1993. If we reclassified as packer-controlled all hogs of the 6 packer controlled operations that went to those packers for slaughter in 1993, the 870,000 head would become 1,793,000 head or 2 percent of national slaughter in 1993. This latter total approximates the total reported in the packer survey.

Large producers marketing in the NCR marketed a higher proportion through open markets -- 26 percent compared to 14 percent for the RON. Conversely, the RON producers marketed 81 percent via forward contracts compared to 63 percent in the NCR.

Projections

These very large hog producers expect a future shift toward closer ties with packers. By 1998, they projected only 10 percent of their MH marketings through spot markets, 73 percent by forward contracts, and 17 percent produced by packers or in joint ventures with them. The number of producers projecting spot transactions dropped in half (from the current 22 to 11). Those projecting use of forward contracts rose from 27 to 33, while those expecting various packer production-slaughter combinations rose from 4 to 7. There were 7 large-size producers that were 100 percent spot market in 1993 that project 100 percent forward contracts by 1998. Four of these seven are headquartered in the NCR and market mainly there.

The projected proportions of these large producers' marketings in 1998 by method and region were as follows:

	NCR	RON	Nation
Open spot markets	11%	10%	10%
Forward contracts	59%	81%	73%
Packer production and joint venture	30%	9%	17%
	100%	100%	100%

Not surprisingly, this projected pattern by region reflects the current regional differences, except for a roughly equal usage of spot markets. Direction of change and approximate magnitude is about all that can be expected from such projections.

Types of Forward Contracts

---

[7]These companies were also interviewed in the packer survey.

Most large producers selling by forward contract receive a formula price based on current market price. Of the 27 producers, 23 had such a formula, 2 had a formula that shared price risk, 1 had a guaranteed floor price, and 1 had a cost of production agreement. Generally, the current price formulas were based on Midwest market prices (terminals and/or direct) plus quality premiums or discounts. An example of sharing price risk is a contract that paid the current market price in the range of $44 to $54 and split 50:50 with the packer on price amounts above or below that range. The floor price guarantee provided current market price or $42 whichever was higher. The cost of production (including a margin for the producer) arrangement seemed much like a production contract, but the packer did not take ownership until the hogs were delivered for slaughter.

Producers with forward contracts reported that 63 percent were written rather than verbal. Likewise, 59 percent were for a fixed contract period (1-15 years) while the other 45 percent continued until canceled.

Fifteen of the 27 producers had a delivery contract with a single packer, while the other 12 had delivery contracts with more than 1 packer. Packers usually had requirements about quality and/or delivery size and timing in these forward contracts. Six contracts required packer approval of the producer line of breeding stock, and 5 others specified minimal quality standards. In 11 cases, a minimal delivery volume was specified: 7 cases specified early morning delivery, 6 asked for projected delivery volumes and dates, and there were a few other variations of these specifications in the forward delivery contracts.

Advantages and Disadvantages of Forward Contracts

The most important benefit producers gave for forward contracts was the assurance of a market outlet (shackle space was the popular term). Reduced market risk came in second in the RON and better prices tied with reduced transaction costs were third. Most important in the NCR was reduced market risk, with reduced transaction costs in second place and assured market outlet ranked third (table 7). A few other reasons such as improved genetics or improved ability to get credit were mentioned. Assured market outlet is important on the East Coast because there are so few packers and packing capacity has been fully utilized in recent years.

Several producers receiving formula prices based on the current market prices cited reduced price risk as a benefit. Perhaps the reasoning is that there is assurance of getting "the market price" without having to search for it.

When producers listed costs and problems associated with forward contracting, 1 of 8 NCR producers said "no costs or problems" while 9 of 17 RON producers said the same. Among the critics there was clear agreement that the inability to shop for better price bids from packers was the chief complaint. Distinctly secondary were a few complaints of reduced flexibility or lower returns (table 8).

Producers listed the primary perceived benefits of forward contracts to packers, as an assured supply of hogs. The NCR producers put lower buying cost as a second benefit and better quality hogs third, while the RON producers reversed those two rankings (table 9). Improving scheduling ranked a distant fourth.

Four of the 9 NCR producers perceived no forward contract costs or disadvantages to packers compared to 6 of the 17 RON producers. There was agreement in both regions that forward contracts might possibly cause packers to pay higher prices at times. A second-rank suggested cost was a loss of some flexibility of operations (table 10).

Feed Company Relationship

"Do you have contracts, joint ventures or other continuing arrangements with one or more commercial feed companies?" Thirty producers answered no, 8 answered yes. Three of these said they were also commercial feed companies, and four said there was a separate feed division operating as a separate profit center in their companies. See table 6 for names of the larger feed- related producers.

The eight producers (including two regional coops) answering yes and another major corporation with a feed division described their feed and hog operation linkages. Six had custom (toll) feed milling arrangements; one producer had a modified custom milling arrangement in which the mill guaranteed to charge only a set margin over the cost of ingredients. Two producers received some financing of facilities plus financing of the feed.

There were only two nonfeed-company producers -- neither very large -- that had financing from feed companies. However, one of those producers has some sort of joint ownership with a large feed dealer. Thus the evidence from large producers indicates that feed company influence is mainly through direct or contract production of hogs rather than by financing large independent producers. The feed companies were reported by these two producers to have no influence over their hog marketing decisions. These two producers said that they obtained more credit than available elsewhere and that they obtained better service from the feed company. Both agreed that the down side of feed company financing was their inability to use other feed suppliers and one mentioned higher feed costs. Both producers ranked the sale of more feed as the primary benefit to the feed company with higher prices or profits second. Of course, higher sales may be consistent with greater profit. One producer perceived no costs and disadvantages to the feed company in financing his hogs, while the other producer suggested greater capital requirements and loss of flexibility.

Contract Finishing

Contractors typically provide feeder pigs, feed, medications, and technical supervision while growers provide the facilities, labor, utilities, and waste disposal. Of the 45 very large producers, 39 reported some hog production contracts. The importance of contract production among the 39 producers ranged from 100 percent of output for some operations to extremely small fractions for others. Of the total hogs contract finished, 2 million or 27 percent were by means of vertical contracting while 5.5 million or 73 percent were by means of horizontal contracts. Thus, horizontal contracting was clearly more important than vertical contracting for these 45 large producers in 1993. Of the marketings of the 5 major feed companies and the 3 packers (not in feed), about 65 percent were finished by contract growers. The 31 non-vertically integrated producers marketed 7.75 million MH, of which 5.5 million were finished by their contract growers and 2.25 million were finished in their own facilities. The six operations with no contract production included two breeding companies which do have contract multipliers for breeding stock, but those multipliers produce and market their own MH (non-breeding stock) from those operations. These 6 operations with no contract production ranged in size from 70,000 MH to more than 500,000 in 1993 and marketed a total of almost 1 million MH.

Of the 21 large producers in the NCR, 16 (76 percent) had contract finishing while 23 of the 24 (96 percent) RON producers contract finished hogs. For all NCR producers, 46 percent of the 1993 MH were contract finished compared to 73 percent of RON producers, an average of 64 percent for both groups.

A considerable variety of finishing contracts were in use in 1993. The seven classifications in table 11 simplify that variety. Certain regional differences can be noted. Note the absence of any profit share contracts except that a cooperative allowed grower members to share in any earnings. The two most common contracts paid fees per head or per pound gained, plus incentives and/or discounts. Incentives (positive or negative) generally involved feed efficiency and sometimes death loss.

These large producer-contractors ranked contracting's benefits as the supplement of available capital, the reduction in (growth of) the hired labor force, good community relations, and facilitating growth (table 12). Of course, the saving on contractor capital is the main way contracting facilities expand so those two benefits could be combined. The general difference in community attitudes toward contract production in the NCR and the RON is illustrated by the regional differences in ranking (table 12).

Contractors in the RON say that the primary downside of contracting is higher costs and lower returns per head while the NCR contractors rank first the additional management problems (table 13). "More risks" was a weak third in both regions.

Contractors cited a variety of benefits to growers in contracting, with no dominant response (table 14). A way to get started or expand, and more income and less risk were among the most frequently stated benefits. There was general agreement by region.

Contractors saw fewer costs, risks, and disadvantages than they saw benefits for growers. One contractor said there were no disadvantages. The absence of any chance of big windfall profits from high hog prices was agreed in both regions to be a primary negative. Nearly as important in the NCR was the loss of independence. That loss was a more distant second in the RON (table 15).

Contractors listed a variety of desirable characteristics of potential growers. Personal characteristics such as energy, dependability, and willingness to learn were most often mentioned (table 16) along with related terms such as well respected, success in previous work, and neatness of home and facilities. Sufficient equity to borrow the necessary capital for facilities was an obvious concern. There were isolated mentions of other factors such as location -- not too close to neighbors and not too far from the contractor.

Contract Farrowing

The primary sources of pigs for the respondents in 1993 were their own facilities or contract growers. The proportions for each region were similar.

NCR	RON	
63%	57%	Pigs produced in own facilities
37	41	Pigs produced by contract growers
0.1	2	Pigs purchased from others
100%	100%	

Thus, about 40 percent of their MH were contract farrowed (occasionally farrow to finish), contrasted with 64 percent that were contract finished. Only 28 large producers had pigs farrowed under contract, while 39 had market hogs finished under contract.

When asked to rank the benefits of contract pig production, almost all respondents replied that the answers were the same as for contract finishing. The same reply was given on the questions about benefits for growers and disadvantages to both the grower and the contractor.

Procurement of Breeding Stock

Producers were asked if they had any contractual or continuing arrangements with sellers of breeding stock. Only six producers -- all in the RON -- said no. Of the 39 others, 6 noted that they were either breeding stock companies or had multiplier units for breeding stock companies. Five of the breeding stock suppliers were in the NCR and one was in the RON. Thus, these 12 were not asked further questions about breeding stock procurement. Among the remaining 33 were 26 producers reporting that they had multiplier herds for their own seedstock. They ordinarily paid a royalty, plus purchase of parents or grandparents, for all breeding stock transferred into their commercial farrowing units. The same proportions of producers in both regions had their own multiplier units.

For the 33 operations purchasing breeding stock under a continuing relationship (including those 26 with their own multiplier herds who pay royalties), we roughly estimate their purchases as 356,000 gilts and 17,000 boars annually.[8]

---

[8] We used a formula to project the probable number of breeding stock added to these herds in 1993 based on their 1993 output and growth from 1992 to 1993. These estimates could easily be wrong in either direction by 10 percent.

Seven producers reported a procurement contract for a fixed period while 25 (11 of the 15 producers in the NCR and 14 of the 17 in the RON) reported an agreement with the source of breeding stock that continued until terminated. The seven fixed period agreements varied widely in length (1-25 years). Twenty-two producers contracted with only 1 supplier of breeding stock in 1993, while 14 (39 percent) producers (6 of the 17 producers in the NCR and 8 of 19 in the RON) had agreements with more than 1 supplier.

Expected Industry Changes -- Next 5 Years

Producers were asked their opinion on the major changes in the next 5 years in who produces hogs and how feed companies and packers would relate to producers. Generally, the 148 responses suggested closer ties among producers and packers, a changing and probably diminishing role for commercial feed companies, more contracting, and more attention to the quality of pork (table 18). No differences in anticipated changes in the two regions were apparent.

Producers were asked for the key benefits and problems that will result for large producers from the expected changes. Producers suggested 59 problems and only 25 benefits. The benefits were generally phrased in industrywide terms although a few producers centered on themselves. The range of opinions about benefits was wide (table 19). Sixteen of the benefits were suggested by NCR producers versus only nine by the RON producers.

Nearly half of the producers listed narrower profit margins as an anticipated problem. A secondary concern was greater environmental problems. Other concerns included the growing power of packers and a variety of managerial problems (table 20).

Of the five respondents of major feed companies, four did not refer to feed companies in answering these two questions on future prospects, while the fifth saw few feed companies in contract production.

Table 6. Partial List of Surveyed Large Producers, 1993

Firm	Headqtrs. State
I. Operations that are not vertically integrated	
Carroll's Food	North Carolina
Murphy	North Carolina
Quarter M[a]	North Carolina
Prestage	North Carolina
National Farms	Missouri
PSF*	Illinois
DeKalb**	Iowa
Farmer's Hybrid**	Kentucky
PIC**	
II. Operations owned or partially controlled by pork packers	
Carroll-Smithfield	North Carolina & Virginia
Cargill+	Minnesota
Farmland+	Missouri
Tyson[b]	Arizona
Seaboard	Kansas
III. Operations owned or partially controlled by feed companies	
Conti Feeds	Illinois
Goldkist	Georgia
Land O' Lakes	Minnesota

*PSF opened a pork packing plant in 1994 in Missouri.
**These are major seedstock producers.
+Cargill and Farmland include both pork packing and feed company divisions.
[a]Quarter M and Murphy were merged in 1994 into Murphy Family Farms.
[b]Tyson in mid 1995 announced sale of its only pork packing plant to Cargill but it remains a major hog producer.

Note: This list includes only firms that are publicly known to be major hog producers within the listed categories. A few more operations in category III, two more in category II, and many more in category I were interviewed.

Table 7. Mean and High Ranks of Perceived Benefits to
Producers of Forward Contracts
for Market Hogs, by Region

Benefits	Number of High Ranks[*]		Mean Ranks[**]	
	NCR	RON	NCR	RON
Assured market outlet (shackle space)	2	13	6.8	3.0
Reduced price risks	7	6	3.0	6.4
Better prices for hogs	0	4	9.0	7.2
Reduced transaction costs	6	6	4.0	7.4
------------------------------	--------	--------	--------	--------
Highest possible score[***]	9	17	1.0	1.0

[*]Number of producers ranking this benefit as first or second.

[**]Ranks run 1 to 9 with 1 as most important and 9 as least. Generally no one gave as many as 9 ranks so the value of 9 was assigned to each benefit not listed by that producer but listed by one or more others. Both counts and means are presented as similar and probably equally valid measures of attributes.

[***]The highest possible count for a particular benefit is equal to the number of producers in a region answering this question, or to the mean rank of 1.0 indicating every respondent ranked it first.

Table 8. Mean and High Ranks of Perceived Costs and Problems to Producers of Forward Contracting Market Hogs, by Region

	Number of 1st & 2nd Ranks		Mean Ranks	
Costs and Problems	NCR	RON	NCR	RON
Prevents shopping for better bids	6	4	3.0	4.4
Reduced flexibility	3	2	6.4	7.0
Lower returns	1	1	8.1	7.9
------------------------------	--------	--------	--------	--------
Highest possible score	7	8	1.0	1.0

Table 9. Mean and High Ranks of Benefits to Packers of Forward Contracts as Perceived by Contracting Producers, by Region

Benefits to Packers	Number of 1st & 2nd Ranks		Mean Ranks	
	NCR	RON	NCR	RON
Secures regular supply of hogs	7	14	1.7	2.1
Lowers buying costs	6	5	4.2	5.9
Obtain better quality hogs	4	9	4.3	4.5
Improved scheduling	1	3	6.2	7.1
------------------------------	--------	--------	--------	--------
Highest possible score	9	17	1.0	1.0

Table 10. Mean and High Ranks of Costs and Disadvantages
of Forward Contracts to Packers as Perceived
by Producers, by Region

Costs and Disadvantages to Packers	Number of 1st & 2nd Ranks		Mean Ranks	
	NCR	RON	NCR	RON
Possibly pay higher prices at times	5	7	1.4	3.9
Lose some flexibility of operations	2	3	4.8	6.9
------------------------------	--------	--------	--------	--------
Highest possible score	5	11	1.0	1.0

Table 11. Relative Usage of the Various Finishing Contracts Based on Number of Producers and on Volume of Hogs Affected, by Region

Contract Type	Percentage of Contractors Using		Percentage of Market Hogs (MH) Covered	
	NCR	RON	NCR	RON
Fee per head marketed	6	13	7	5
Fee per head marketed plus incentives	38	39	37	19
Fee per pound of gain	6	4	1	3
Fee per pound of gain plus incentives	31	39	46	44
Cash rent plus fee per pound of gain plus incentives	6	0	*	0
Fee per space used plus incentives	6	4	5	29
Cost per pound of gain	6	0	4	0
Total Percentage	99	99	100	100

*Approximately ½ percent.

Table 12. Mean and High Ranks of Perceived Benefits of Contract Production to the Contractors, by Region

Benefits to Contractors	Number of 1st & 2nd Ranks		Mean Ranks	
	NCR	RON	NCR	RON
Supplements capital	16	22	1.2	1.6
Reduces need for hired labor	5	6	5.7	5.8
Good community relations	2	7	7.6	6.3
Facilitates expansion	5	6	6.4	6.8
------------------------------	--------	--------	--------	--------
Highest possible score	16	23	1.0	1.0

Table 13. Mean and High Ranks of Perceived Cost, Risks, and Disadvantages to the Contractors of Contracting, by Region

Costs, Risks and Disadvantages to Contractors	Number of 1st & 2nd Ranks		Mean Ranks	
	NCR	RON	NCR	RON
Higher costs and lower returns	7	19	5.6	2.7
More management problems	9	13	3.9	4.4
More risks	3	5	7.6	7.2
------------------------------	--------	--------	--------	--------
Highest possible score	16	23	1.0	1.0

Table 14. Mean and High Ranks of Contracting Benefits to Growers as Perceived by Contractors, by Region

Contracting Benefits to Growers	Number of 1st & 2nd Ranks		Mean Ranks	
	NCR	RON	NCR	RON
Allows producers to start or to grow	9	11	4.2	4.5
Reduced price risks	8	6	4.9	5.8
More certain returns	6	8	5.8	4.8
Supplements income	4	8	6.7	5.3
More income and/or improves cash flow	3	6	6.5	6.3
Simplifies their management	1	6	6.8	6.1
-------------------------------	--------	--------	--------	--------
Highest possible score	16	23	1.0	1.0

Table 15. Mean and High Ranks of Contracting Costs, Risks, and Disadvantages to Growers as Perceived by Contractors, by Region

Costs, Risks and Disadvantages to Growers	Number of 1st & 2nd Ranks		Mean Ranks	
	NCR	RON	NCR	RON
No chance of big returns	12	16	3.4	3.4
Less independence	11	9	3.4	5.3
Risk of losing contract	4	8	6.3	6.3
------------------------------	--------	--------	--------	--------
Highest possible score	16	22	1.0	1.0

Table 16. Characteristics of Growers Sought by Large Contractors:
Mean and High Ranks by Region

Characteristics of Growers	Number of 1st & 2nd Ranks		Mean Ranks	
	NCR	RON	NCR	RON
Dependability	6	10	5.4	4.8
Energetic and hard-working	9	8	4.8	5.6
Sufficient equity to finance facilities	5	6	3.8	5.4
Good references	3	5	7.3	6.4
Willingness to learn	4	2	6.8	7.5
------------------------------	--------	--------	--------	--------
Highest possible score	16	23	1.0	1.0

Table 17. Mean Ranks of Benefits to Contractors of
Contract Finishing and Contract Farrowing

	Benefit Mean Ranks	
Benefits	Finishing	Farrowing
Supplements available capital	1.4	1.2
Reduces need to hire labor	8.0	5.4
Good community relations	6.8	6.3
Facilitates expansion	6.6	7.0

Table 18. Various Industry Changes Expected by Large Producers in Next 5 Years

Anticipated Changes	Number of Producers Mentioning
Big producers get bigger	25
More marketing contracts with packers	23
More vertical integration of producers and packers	14
More production contracts by packers	10
More mergers of packers	5
More packer direction of production	6
Some producers try to get into packing	2
Feed companies shrink	13
Feed companies produce hogs to save a role	10
Feed companies may need to provide more services	11
Continued emphasis on better genetics	10
Production more consumer driven	6
More contract production	7
More producer networks	4
Lower cost of production	2
TOTAL	148

Table 19. Specific Benefits Expected by Large Producers from
Anticipated Industry Changes in Next 5 Years

Anticipated Benefits	Number of Producers Mentioning
Improved product quality and market acceptance	9
More efficient production	5
More rapid transfer of information and technology	4
More efficient pricing system	2
Better access to capital	2
More opportunity to contract production among smaller producers	1
Will strengthen my operation	1
Can get more technical resources as I grow	1
TOTAL	25

Table 20. Specific Problems Expected by Large Producers from Anticipated Industry Changes in Next 5 Years

Anticipated Problems	Number of Producers Mentioning
Tighter margins (less profit per head)	20
More environmental problems (regulation)	13
Less independence in a more vertically aligned system	6
More restricted access to packers and less competition among them	5
More opposition to corporate farming	4
Concerns whether I can continue to compete	4
Scarcity of quality labor and hired management	4
Will need to get bigger and sell by contract	1
Quality of management will become more critical	1
Can I get enough long-term loans?	1
TOTAL	59

Large Feed Company Survey

Twenty-one of the Nation's 22 largest feed manufacturers were surveyed regarding their activities in and perceptions of the vertical coordination alliances occurring in the U.S. pork industry. Feed Management magazine (December 1993) was the source of the population to be surveyed (table 21). Three large feed companies did not have annual hog feed sales in excess of 15,000 tons, and were not interviewed further since they had little commercial involvement with the pork industry. Five large feed companies were part of the companion study of large pork producers; managers of the feed divisions of four of these firms were surveyed (in addition to their hog ownership divisions, reported earlier) to get the feed division perspective on the changes in the industry. Individuals interviewed within the 18 companies responding to the survey included the CEO, sales or swine products managers, or other upper level management directly involved in the firm's decisions regarding their swine industry involvement.

The 18 companies interviewed can be classified into 3 basic groups: national firms, regional firms, and farmer-owned cooperatives. The hog feed trade area closely matches the geographical distribution of hog production -- the Corn Belt, east central and southeastern U.S. regional firms and cooperatives (a distinction used later) were located in either the Corn Belt or the east-southeast, while national feed companies were found in both. Although some companies did not disclose information about either total feed sales volume or the share that was hog feed, the annual hog feed volume of those responding ranged from 20,000 to over 200,000 tons.

With the exception of the four companies interviewed that are among the largest hog producers in the country, very few of the other feed companies surveyed reported that they currently produced hogs either in their own facilities or under contract (with the exception of research farms). Only three firms did not offer some type of credit package to dealers or hog producers. In spite of the wide range of financing available, over 70 percent of hog feed was sold on a cash basis to dealers or directly to the hog producer.

Financing Programs

The feed companies offered three basic types of financing: short-term (30-60 days) credit extension, ongoing working capital, or financing of a single group of pigs. There were some differences in feed company managers' perception of what constitutes financing. Three firms considered payment not made in 10 days as a credit extension. Four of the firms offered only one financing program, such as financing only feed. Three firms offered two financing programs (feed and other variable inputs) and seven firms offered three or more financing programs. Seven of the 18 feed companies indicated that financing was tied to a specific group of hogs being fed. While this financing was typically only for feed, some feed companies would also finance feeder pigs. Seven of the companies offered continuous financing or a rolling credit account, typically for working capital, while some were offering long-term financing for facilities. In some cases, financing was provided to the feed dealer but not to the hog producer. Dealers may also be providing credit to hog producers.

All financing programs required a formal written agreement between the borrower and the feed company to reduce the risk of non-payment. Increased risk exposure was often cited as a disadvantage of feed company financing programs. No financing agreements required hog producers to use specific genetics or breeding stock suppliers. Two respondents reported that the financing agreements allowed them to select marketing dates and outlets; this was intended to protect their secured interest in the hogs and reduce their risk exposure rather than the desire to coordinate the marketing channel.

Although nearly all firms offered financing of feed and possibly other variable inputs, less than a third of the firms offered financing of hog production facilities. However, many remarked that they were considering financing facilities in the future. All but two respondents expected that an increased proportion of their future feed sales would be tied to their current financing program or an expanded version.

Advantages and Disadvantages of Financing Programs

The major benefit of financing programs reported by 12 feed companies was selling more feed (table 22). The additional sales arose from helping their customers grow, which in turn leads to more feed sales, or by acquiring new customers who may not have access to other sources of credit. Less frequently mentioned responses included closer ties of the producer to the company, better future positioning, utilizing economies of size, responding to competition, and support of their dealer network.

The primary disadvantages reported by feed companies (table 23) were their increased risks due to unpaid receivables (8) and the need for greater capital requirements (6). A few firms cited increased cost of selling feed (4) and less profitable use of capital (4) as additional disadvantages.

Benefits perceived by the feed company for the recipient of feed company financing, while expressed in several ways, centered around increased access to credit (table 24). Specific benefits included more credit, better terms, less paper work and regulation than conventional lenders, and convenience of payments and record keeping. The feed companies indicated that greater access to capital allowed producers to expand their hog operations, use existing capital in other areas of the operation, and improve their financial statements. Although not commonly reported, a few firms thought that feed companies understood modern pork production better than most lenders, and that producers received better financial and management services from the feed company when it was financially involved.

Few disadvantages of feed company financing were perceived for the producer (table 25). Only 11 disadvantages were given compared to 28 advantages. Disadvantages included the loss of producer flexibility (4), higher interest rates (4), and higher feed costs (2). The perception of higher interest rates by some respondents could be viewed as inconsistent with the perceived advantage of better credit terms by others. This difference may be a consequence of different interest rates offered by some feed companies or attributable to the fact that credit terms typically involve more than just rates.

Future Direction of Financing Programs

Ten companies currently offering financing to hog producers expected to expand the volume of feed sold through such programs in the future, while 2 companies thought that their volume of financed feed would not increase. Nearly all respondents indicated that financing arrangements by feed companies would increase in the next 5 years. Seven believed that contract arrangements tying the hog producer to a packer or feed company or both would be necessary to secure financing in the future. Three expected an increase in long-term financing for hog production facilities. In general, the feed companies thought that the use of non-traditional sources of credit such as investment banks, international banks, mutual funds, etc., by hog producers would increase.

Future Direction of the Hog Industry -- Next Five Years

Fourteen feed companies indicated that there would be more linkages among feed companies, producers, packers, and possibly breeding stock companies in the future. These forecasts ranged from simply more formal coordination among participants in the production and marketing channels to vertical integration through ownership of all phases of production and marketing. Six companies anticipated stronger linkages, and five companies expected that there would be more information sharing.

Twelve companies specifically stated that hog production units would be larger and six noted that hog production and management would be more specialized. Two respondents projected an increased demand for complete feed from feed companies as hog producers become more specialized and contract out feed preparation and delivery. Several respondents indicated that feed company margins would be narrower, and that feed companies would have to provide more sophisticated services in order to earn their margins. The increased services include more tailored research, information collection and analysis, and providing assistance in managerial decisions and problem solving.

Some feed company managers expected that the hog industry will become more segmented, and that each segment will have different needs. Traditional diversified Midwest hog farms are a shrinking share of the feed market. Financing by feed companies appears to be a non-price competition response in an attempt to salvage or gain a larger share of this shrinking market. The growing market is by larger producers who are placing greater demands upon feed companies. In particular, very large producers may have their own feed mill, and may provide their own feed milling and delivery services. Feed companies may be asked to provide more specialized services such as: nutritional research tailored to a production firms' specific genetic lines, facilities, and climate; information management and analysis of relationships among nutrition, genetics, and product quality; logistics of input purchasing and handling; mill management and mill employee training; and ingredient quality control. Although contrary to the general perception that there is overcapacity in the feed milling sector, one feed company indicated that new mills would be built dedicated to hog feed rather than trying to make use of current excess capacity in outdated mills to supply this more specialized market.

Benefits and Challenges to Feed Companies

Common themes among the feed companies surveyed were that the future holds tighter margins for feed companies, increased specialization of diets and programs geared to specific genetic lines, and the need to provide more sophisticated products and services such as financing, research, and information transfer services for clients. Three companies indicated that the increased services and research would facilitate more customer loyalty. If a diet was developed specifically for an individual producer's needs, the producer would be less likely to switch companies.

The industry also faces challenges of increased government regulation of products and procedures regarding food safety, Hazard Analysis Critical Control Point policies, and more rapidly changing technology. Individual firms are challenged to segment their customers and provide the inputs that each segment needs and wants. All respondents acknowledged that there would be fewer customers in the future. Specifically, two companies predicted that there would be only five major feed companies in the future. Few firms offered their strategy as to how they may be one of the remaining firms. Although some feed companies have begun producing hogs as a way to secure tonnage for their mill or as a profit center, others have advertised that they will not feed hogs in competition with their customers.

Hog Production by Feed Companies

Four of the feed companies surveyed are among the largest hog producers and their information is included in that section of this report. The feed and hog production divisions of these companies are managed as separate profit centers. The feed division managers see a trend to both increased consolidation and coordination in the pork sector. The companies have segmented the hog feed market. Although the hog production divisions continue to grow, the feed divisions continue to try to help their feed customers compete with integrators. They see managing information and developing relationships between producers and processors or other input suppliers as services to assist producers and secure feed sales. There does not appear to be an attempt to short-change feed customers in order to further the hog production part of the firm.

Three feed companies that are not among the largest hog producers reported that they owned hogs. One indicated that it produced hogs in its own facilities and two reported producing hogs in contract facilities. Total 1994 combined production for the three firms was expected to be less than 200,000 head.

Companies who are not currently large hog producers were asked how many hogs their company would own in 1998. Five responded that they would not own hogs. Four indicated sharp increases from their current level, but relatively small production levels by modern standards. Three indicated that they will likely own some hogs, with the volume depending on the evolution of corporate farming laws and the success of their current pilot projects.

Summary and Overview

Large feed companies appear to have decided to either be a major player in hog production (five are among the largest U.S. producers) or not to produce any significant numbers of hogs. The larger firms that made a commitment to own hogs appear to manage and operate hog production and feed divisions as separate profit centers, so there are few synergies from being in both businesses. While the initial motivation for producing hogs may have been to increase internally generated feed sales, the profit potential in hog production appears to be the primary driving force to own hogs.

The financing agreements used by feed companies are a non-price-competitive strategy to maintain or increase market share. While the capital provided may marginally influence the number of hogs produced, these arrangements usually have little influence on the coordination linkages of pork producers with processors or other input suppliers.

While they are preparing to service larger producers, assist management, and help them develop horizontal and vertical linkages, vertical integration by feed companies is a relatively minor driving force stimulating coordination system changes in the hog sector.

Table 21. The 22 Largest Commercial Feed Companies in the U.S. -- 1993

Company	Headquarters
Cargill/Nutrena	Minneapolis, MN
Purina Mills	St. Louis, MO
Gold Kist, Inc.	Atlanta, GA
Kent Feeds, Inc.	Muscatine, IA
Land O' Lakes	Arden Hills, MN
PM Ag Products	Homewood, IL
Central-Soya Co., Inc.	Ft. Wayne, IN
Farmland Industries	Kansas City, MO
Coast Grain Co.	Ontario, CA
Continental Grain Co.	Chicago, IL
Moorman Mfg. Co.	Quincy, IL
Supersweet Feeds-AgP, L.P.	Omaha, NE
Hubbard Milling Co.	Mankato, MN
Agway, Inc.	Syracuse, NY
O.H. Kruse Grain and Milling	Ontario, CA
Southern States	Richmond, VA
Harvest States Cooperative	St. Paul, MN
SF Services, Inc.	Little Rock, AR
Golden Sun Feeds, Inc.	Estherville, IA
Countrymark	Indianapolis, IN
MFA, Inc.	Columbia, MO
United Feeds	Sheridan, IN

Source: <u>Feed Management Magazine,</u> December 1993.

Table 22. Perceived Benefits to Feed Company of Financing Feed and/or Hog Production

	Total	Rankings (No. of Responses)		
		1	2	3
Sells more feed	12	12		
Ties producer to company	5	1	3	1
Helps customer grow	3	1	1	
Improves cash flow for dealers	2		2	
Obtains economies of size	1		1	
Keep up with competition	1		1	
Revenue source	1		1	
Positions for future	1		1	
Sells better quality feed	1			1
Firm better understands customer	1			1

Table 23. Perceived Disadvantages to Feed Company of Financing Feed and/or Hog Production

	Total	Rankings (No. of Responses)		
		1	2	3
Increases risk	8	6	2	
Requires more capital	6	6		
Lower profits than other uses of capital	4	1	3	
Increases expense of selling feed	4		3	1
Producer resentment of financing competitor	1	1		
Get producer to provide financial information	1		1	
Possible environmental liability	1			1

Table 24. Perceived Benefits for Hog Producers of Feed Company Financing Feed and/or Hog Production

	Total	Rankings (No. of Responses)			
		1	2	3	4
Obtain better credit terms	3		3		
Allows expansion of hog production	4	3		1	
Convenience of payment	3	1	1		1
Easier to get credit	2		2		
Often more credit available	6	3	1	2	
Improve cash flow	1	1			
Obtain better feed company service	1	1			
Improve credit availability for other operation	1	1			
Able to get dealer discounts and financing	1	1			
Work with knowledgeable pork lender	1	1			
Lender that understands modern hog production	1	1			
More consistent source of funds	1		1		
Improve financial statement	1		1		
Obtain better facilities	1			1	
Convenience of closeout records	1				1

Table 25. Perceived Costs or Disadvantages for Hog Producers of Feed Company Financing Feed and/or Hog Production

	Total	Rankings (No. of Responses)		
		1	2	3
Loss of flexibility	4	4		
Higher than market interest rate	4	3	1	
Higher feed cost	2	2		
May not be local lender	1		1	

An Integrated Analysis

Packer-Larger Producers Long-Term Marketing Contract Rationale

Most of the long-term (LT) contracts were not fixed price; rather price was based upon a reported market(s), usually on Midwest reported prices, at time of delivery. Such contracts generally were not shifting price risk to packers. These large producers are generally quite entrepreneurial and quite willing to assume price risks. Whether a year or more of hog prices as low as those experienced in the fall of 1994 will increase their demand for risk-sharing contracts remains to be seen.

Usage of LT forward marketing contracts was highly related to the size of the producer. The total volume of hogs in such contracts for these 45 large producers roughly equaled the reported volume of 19 of the Nation's 20 largest packers (8.7 and 8.4 million head, respectively). This equality implies that these packers' contracts were almost entirely with these large producers. Given the 86.5 percent of national commercial slaughter handled by the surveyed packers, there was little room for much contracting elsewhere. In the unlikely case that the excluded -- and mostly smaller -- packers contracted as high a percentage as the surveyed packers, that would add another 1.3 million market hogs sold via LT contracts between those excluded packers and smaller producers.

Not only were most large packer LT forward contracts with these large producers but there was also a strong relation to size of producer within this group of 45. Each of 7 mega-producers marketed more than 500,000 hogs per year or more than 2,000 per day (based on 250 marketing days per year). The marketings of the other 38 ranged from 62,000 up to about 350,000 or from 250 to 1,400 per day. Only 1 percent of the 7 mega-producers volume was sold through the spot market, with 90 percent on LT contracts and 9 percent directly packer controlled or production contract. In contrast, the 38 smaller producers had 41 percent of their MH sold through the spot market, 53 percent by LT marketing contracts, and 6 percent was packer controlled.

Why is the size of the producer such a factor in their avoidance of open markets? Most plants do not normally slaughter more than 10,000 per day. Thus, a mega-producer selling 2,000 to 4,000 hogs per day can supply a significant fraction of a typical plant's daily output. All mega- producers in North Carolina ranked assured shackle space as the first or second most important benefit of LT contracts, as did 9 of the 13 other large producers in North Carolina and other areas outside the NCR. In contrast, only 1 of the 3 mega-producers in the NCR and only 1 of 6 of the other large industry producers in it ranked assured shackle space as either first or second as a benefit of LT contracts. Industry sources report that packers in North Carolina are less tolerant of producers shopping around than is the case in other regions. Long-term contracts reduce the risk that producers could be cut off by packers in the short run.

Neither the very large producer nor the nearby packers want the disruption of efficient operations associated with shopping around on a daily basis if they can come to some long-term accommodation. Several packers noted consistency of supplies or increased numbers of hogs as advantages of long-term contracts. Vulnerability to short-term opportunism on the other side of the market might be greatest for very large producers outside the NCR (Williamson's specific assets theory), yet it also can have a major influence on packers who frequently have excess capacity and a downward sloping cost curve as plant volume increases. This suggests as producers become larger and the regional packing industry becomes more concentrated, less reliance on the open market would be anticipated.

In the Southeast, these major ties of supplies by LT forward contracts -- and to a much smaller extent by production contracts, etc. -- reduce the volume of hogs bought in daily competition by the two major packers and simplifies their daily interaction although not necessarily their degree of competition. In fact, Smithfield's recent huge expansion of capacity has moved it into a leading position in the packer group.

There are other benefits of LT contracts. The savings in transaction costs over the spot market from dealing in large lots are minor for the packer -- at most, 50 cents per cwt. Large producers also reduce transaction costs through LT contracts although less than packers do. Packers generally state that an assured large volume alone will not receive a price premium although we suspect some packer sharing of these small savings with very large producers.

There is also some quality assurance since supplies from a given producer should not shift quickly over time. A large producer can settle his premium on quality with one-time negotiation of contract terms. For a packer in an area of short supplies, a contract may be a device for increasing procurement share and/or total area supplies; such contracting was a factor for broiler processors during the transition from open markets to integration. Only 8 of the 19 packers purchased 10 percent or more of their hogs via LT marketing contracts, so the benefits to packers -- especially in the NCR -- are apparently less than overwhelming. Since there was much higher participation by large producers than by packers in LT contracts, the incentives can be presumed to be greater for large producers, especially outside the NCR, than for packers.

In summary, LT marketing contracts can benefit packers and producers by small savings in transaction costs and by aiding quality improvement. Moreover, in packer markets -- especially oligopsonistic ones -- LT contracts may reduce the uncertainties of day-to-day procurement and may help increase a packer's procurement share. Marketing contracts can benefit producers by small savings in transaction costs, by settling the terms of rewards for quality, and in oligopsonistic markets, by reducing the risks of packer opportunism in daily purchases. The much greater shares of LT marketing contracts on the part of larger rather than smaller producers suggest that large producers find the advantages more significant. Large packer projections of LT contract volume in 1998 aggregated to 20 million head, while very large producer projections totaled 21.6 million. While most LT marketings contracts are with very large producers, we anticipate increased LT contracts with intermediate size producers as well. Thus, the larger packers' projection of an increase in LT contracts to 25 percent of their volume in 5 years is probably conservative.

Vertical Integration -- Packing and Hog Production

The reported total volume of packer-controlled output at 1.8 million head matched the same total for the large producers using the broadest definition of packer-control. There were five cases of packer-producer vertical integration (VI) with significant volume including Tyson's recent purchase of a slaughter plant in 1993, PSF opening a plant in late 1994, and Seaboard building a plant scheduled to open in 1995 to be supplied mainly by its controlled production.

In looking at causation, it is important to distinguish between two situations: (1) packers Smithfield and Seaboard that have integrated into production and (2) large-scale hog producers PSF, Cargill, and Tyson that have integrated into packing. A development of their case histories using public information will show both similarities and differences in motivating factors between and within these two groups.

Vertical Integration of Two Packers Into Hog Production

Seaboard, a conglomerate, entered meat packing by buying an old plant in Minnesota a few years ago. About 2 years later, it began contract production of hogs in Colorado. Seaboard will be using contract production to help supply a new plant it is building in the Oklahoma Panhandle, where there is not nearly enough production to run a modern plant. It has not shared its reasons for that location. One can speculate that interest in a pork market in Mexico, a belief that large-scale production was very profitable, and a conviction that large-scale hog production could be built much more rapidly in those wide open spaces (due to arid climate, sparse population, and support of state and local economic development groups) may have all been factors. Seaboard may have enlarged its toehold entry as a new packer more easily by its Oklahoma venture than by trying to buy a larger procurement share in established hog production areas in the NCR. Once it chose to enter an area of limited production such as western Oklahoma, it was less risky to build simultaneously both hog production and a packing plant.

Smithfield, the East Coast packer with a significant amount of hog production, has 2 small plants in southeast Virginia, and a huge new plant in North Carolina. They slaughter a majority of the rapidly rising hog production in a state that has been significantly increasing its share of national output in the past decade. Ten years ago, Smithfield was bringing in hogs from the NCR to slaughter. Now its controlled production through two jointly owned large producers in North Carolina and Virginia reduces its risk of being short of hogs to slaughter. Moreover, many of its hog purchases involve LT contracts with major producers in North Carolina. Its day-to-day procurement risks probably have been reduced. Since profits in hog production and packing are negatively associated over the hog cycle, Smithfield may appreciate the risk diversification of VI. The information about production costs obtained in its joint ventures may be useful in its negotiation of premiums over Midwest market prices paid in its LT marketing contracts. It has indicated publicly that the main attraction of own hog production has been its great profitability. Smithfield has publicly proclaimed VI as the wave of the future.

Smithfield recently joined with three major North Carolina producers to form Circle Four, a firm that has started hog production in Utah and plans to build enough production there to justify a new slaughter plant in that same valley by 1998.

Smithfield has used both LT contracts and VI to utilize more fully its packing capacity and become the dominant packer in North Carolina. Both have helped its quest for better quality. Its participation in Circle Four involves setting up both production and packing in an isolated area lacking both; VI is the practical way to solve the chicken-and-egg problem of production before packing or vice versa. Seaboard's entry into VI in the Oklahoma Panhandle has the same characteristics as Circle Four.

To what extent have quality concerns motivated packers into VI? Packers have generally had more information than producers; packers have had considerable ability to select desired qualities from a heterogenous quality mix without necessarily paying fully for the better qualities. It is becoming conventional wisdom that quality (leanness, and yet good appearance and palatability) is becoming the driving force. However, very little evidence has been presented. Quality has long been given lip service but little action by packers. Some exceptionally high- quality processors such as Hormel have not integrated vertically. However, the increasing Japanese market for high-quality cuts and interest in developing quality brand differentiation may be stimulating some real changes in packer plans and behavior.

The reasons for packer-producer integration have been more varied than transaction cost theory would suggest. Our first and most important point is that little of this **packer initiated** VI would have occurred absent large profits for progressive large-scale hog production. It is not unusual when capital is flowing rapidly into an industry to utilize new technologies that some of it comes from allied firms; in this case from packers. In our opinion, the motive of capturing profits in modern, large-scale hog production has dominated Williamson's rationale for vertical integration.

Vertical Integration of Three Large Producers Into Packing

PSF began hog production in Missouri in 1989 intending to do its own farrowing and contract for finishing. It soon became clear that grower recruitment could not possibly keep up with its rapid expansion of farrowing. So it does virtually all of its own finishing. By 1995, PSF will be producing 1.6 million hogs annually, and will be slaughtering them in a plant opened in late 1994 in northern Missouri near its production sites. PSF has stressed a strong interest in pork quality which helps explain why it as a leading producer went to VI. It can save transportation costs by not hauling to Iowa plants and it may have had long-term concerns about the competitiveness for hogs it might experience among nearby packers if it did not do its own packing. By building a three-county production site and a packing plant exactly scaled to that level of production, PSF can use all facilities quite efficiently.

Tyson was already a leading producer and processor of broilers when it became a hog producer. Tyson began hog production to utilize waste feed from its broilers, found it profitable, gradually expanded, and, nearly 20 years later, purchased a packing plant in Missouri nearly 200 miles north of its nearest production. Tyson is now pursuing a center-of-the-plate merchandising strategy that will involve distributing all the meats, making it fully integrated from feed mill through wholesale distribution. Tyson has generally excelled as a merchandiser, and the use of a packing plant to service that activity more smoothly and reliably appeared to complement its need to find an outlet for its growing hog production, which is now about half of the plant's capacity. However, in 1995, Tyson announced the sale of its packing plant to Cargill. It would appear that Tyson did not find its vertical integration into pork packing to be very profitable.

As the Nation's largest agribusiness conglomerate, Cargill operates many divisions. Its feed division entered hog production in 1973 in Arkansas because it had excess feed mill capacity in an area where poultry contracting had made that institution understood and acceptable. There was too little independent hog production in the area for its expansion to be an option. Cargill found contract production profitable and expanded it in North Carolina and eventually elsewhere. Cargill generally has used its own mills for feed and less often its own packing plants for outlets. Risk diversification may be important to those allocating capital within Cargill although it is of no direct interest to the manager of the hog division, who is judged on the profits generated in it.

After Cargill began hog production in 1973, it purchased a large beef packer (now known as Excel) in 1979 and purchased its first pork plant in 1987. The possible economies of scope in merchandising pork with beef may have been a motive for entering pork packing. Gradually, much of its Arkansas and Missouri hog production has been transferred to its NCR pork plants, but its North Carolina hogs do not go to its NCR packing plants. This territorial distinction may provide a rough measure of the advantages of VI; the absence of VI for its North Carolina hogs suggests that extra transportation costs offset savings in other transaction costs and other benefits such as coordination of quantity and quality in production and packing that are probably gained for its Arkansas and Missouri produced hogs.

Getting an adequate premium for quality in the open market has long been a problem for producers. PSF, as a producer initiator of VI, appears able to reduce transaction (especially transportation) costs and to enhance its merchandising of pork through control of quantity and quality of its hog supplies. Thus, PSF's producer VI into packing conforms rather well with the Williamson model of quality improvement and reduction of transaction costs.

Large-scale hog producers appear more profitable than small operators, based on relative growth rates and limited information on comparative costs of production. And profits from hog production have been a driving force for some integrators. This short-run situation of high profits for one segment of hog producers with low profits or losses for other segments will eventually be changed through continued expansion of the more profitable techniques and firms and the exiting of the less profitable. However, we expect this disequilibrium situation will prevail for at least 10 years, so it will continue to be a force for change in industry and coordination systems.

It follows that the extent of increase in VI in the next 5 to 10 years will depend partly on the extent to which packers -- including producer-packers like PSF -- expand hog production more rapidly than do independent hog producers. That race partly depends on the extent to which hog production expands into new areas such as Utah, Oklahoma and Texas where the absence of packers encourages VI. There is a penalty of about 2 to 3 cents per pound of pork due to higher feed costs in such feed deficit areas. However, costs of waste handling may compensate -- particularly if local opposition to waste and associated odors continues to escalate in the NCR and even in North Carolina. Large expansion in the West and Southwest in arid, lightly populated areas would drive out less competitive producers in the NCR and might lead packers there to turn to contracts to keep up procurement volumes. Whether such strategies would be very successful in areas that are becoming hostile to hog operations (no hog odors in our neighborhood) is not clear. We cannot predict with much confidence the relative expansion outside the currently important production areas. Thus, corresponding predictions about the growth in VI are subject to high error. The packers' prediction of a doubling of their share of VI hogs (to 5.2 million head) in the next 5 years is probably conservative. Large producers predicted an increase of approximately the same -- to 5.0 million head. We can construct scenarios where expansion would be faster. However, we would consider 10 million head under packer VI by 1998 to be the upper limit.

Horizontal Versus Vertical Contracting in the Future

Which will expand faster? Several major uncertainties interact to plague the forecaster. First, we have already discussed the question of how fast packers will enter and/or expand hog production relative to large contractors and independents. Second, even if packers expand faster, they may use joint ventures with little or no production contracting. Joint ventures spread risk and permit a packer to participate in hog production without acquiring a set of skills and technologies very different from those essential in packing. Third, the recruitment of growers has mostly been slow and difficult in the NCR outside the few areas where poultry contracting has been experienced. As noted, PSF abandoned horizontal contracting in the NCR as too slow. If the rate of expansion that has characterized the leaders in hog production in the period 1990-94 resumes after the slowdown expected in 1995, contracting of any kind may not expand as rapidly as the large producers' own production. This point seems paradoxical because a primary appeal of production contracting outside the NCR in the 1970s and 1980s had been the increased size and speed of expansion possible with a given amount of equity capital. That advantage may still hold in North Carolina and the Southeast, but perhaps not in many other areas. The wide experience with poultry contracts on the part of lenders and potential growers certainly facilitated the growth of hog contracting in North Carolina which, in turn, facilitated rapid growth of the early leaders, which sparked numerous imitators that are now very large producers. Fourth, a rising tide of environmental complaints voiced by potential neighbors of new hog operations in many areas may itself slow the speed of expansion. Fifth, the income losses for hog producers occurring recently and probably during much of 1995 may slow considerably the inflow of capital for a few years beyond. Probably such a slowdown would give more advantage to contracting as it is an institution that stretches major producers' capital.

Structure, Conduct, and Performance of the Pork Production Sector

Within the NCR, where about 80 percent of hogs have long been produced, the producer side of the industry approximates the purely competitive model. More than 100,000 small and intermediate-size producers offer a commodity to a dozen or more competing buyers. Information is hardly perfect since each packer has his/her own system of rewarding quality of a commodity and none of these reward systems is entirely transparent. The few very large producers in the NCR often use marketing contracts; this practice leaves small producers wondering if there is favoritism. However, on the whole, this market is generally quite competitive. Packing margins historically have been very thin, and hog prices respond quickly to changes in supplies and demand. It is only in times of heavy hog runs when the producer demand for packing-house services presses hard upon the supply -- as was true in the fall of 1994 -- that packing margins soar, and this behavior is consistent with the purely competitive model. In the NCR, while IBP is clearly the largest packer, the CR-4 (the market share accounted for by the largest 4 packers) is below the level associated with significant market power unless quite restricted geographic areas are considered to be discrete markets for hogs.

If the Southeast, the largest production area outside the NCR, is considered as a distinct hog market, it essentially has a packer oligopsony--with Smithfield by far the largest buyer. The largest producers that each market 3,000 or more hogs per day are not as easily intimidated as the smaller producers, but it is clear that they do not hold an edge in bargaining power over Smithfield. Of course, Smithfield lacks significant market power in sales since it sells pork in a national market. It has only a limited price range in which it can exercise buying power without causing hogs to be shipped elsewhere. In fact, some hogs are shipped to slaughter in Pennsylvania, and Murphy reaches Midwest markets by shipping some feeder pigs to Iowa for finishing and sale there. Smithfield has not sought the quiet life of oligopsonistic restraints; rather it has moved aggressively to increase its market share in hog packing, suggesting from a dynamic Schumpeterian view that its conduct has generally been competitive up to this time. There are numerous smaller producers in the North Carolina area producing fewer total hogs than the very large producers. As noted, these producers have complained about the levels of local market prices and some are said to have concerns about shackle space.

In summary, the producer side of hog markets is quite competitive. The packer-buying side of the market is also workably competitive for the most part with any concerns centering in areas characterized by location-related market power such as the Southeast. On the whole, the low profit margins of slaughter operations have been consistent with a workably competitive industry.

The structure of production is in the midst of sweeping change. It is quite possible that, by the year 2000, 25 to 35 percent of output will come from 100 to 200 large producers (2,500 plus sows) and that a few producers will each be marketing 3 to 5 million head. It seems probable that a growing share of this large-scale production will be in the NCR. Such changes in the NCR will pressure the existing behavior and structure of the packing firms in the NCR. More dependence upon LT contracting and also upon VI can be expected. The industry is entering an unstable and uncertain period; numerous structural configurations could result, depending upon various business and governmental decisions.

Marketing Contracts and Vertical Integration Impacts

LT contracts and ownership VI have not been extensive enough to expect impacts in the NCR, but they have had some impact in the Southeast. Structural effects have been small. Packer VI and usage of LT contracts made rapid growth in packing capacity less risky and contributed to a little more concentration among producers. It is possible that VI and LT contracts have made entry by another packer more difficult, by restricting the potential supply of hogs, but we cannot take for granted that there would have been entry absent the LT contracts and VI, or that entry will not occur in the future.

It is possible that improved packer-producer communication about quality (including a better premium structure) has contributed to pricing and resource efficiency including a more rapid adjustment of producers. It is also possible that these extensive ties of packers and big producers with their prices typically tied to the Midwest markets have brought pressure on the smaller producers selling in local North Carolina markets. There have been considerable local protests about the local markets diverging far too far below Midwest prices. However, quality variations would need to be known to appraise the validity of such complaints. Moreover, the high concentration of buyers in the Southeast, in itself, is very likely to raise producers fears. And this concentration may stimulate entry by competitors, such as IBP, who in 1995 announced plans for a North Carolina plant. If there have been any discernible impacts of VC and VI upon consumers, they are likely to have been positive -- total supplies of pork may be greater and consumer prices lower.

References

Azzam, A.M. and A.C. Wellman. 1992. <u>Packer Integration into Hog Production: Current Status and Likely Impacts of Increased Vertical Control on Hog Prices and Quantities</u>. Lincoln: University of Nebraska Agricultural Research Bulletin 315-F.

Barry, Peter J., Steven T. Sonka, and Kaouthar Lajili. 1992. "Vertical Coordination, Financial Structure and the Changing Theory of the Firm." <u>American Journal of Agricultural Economics,</u> Vol. 74, No. 5, pp. 1219-1225.

Breimyer, Harold F. 1962. "The Three Economies of Agriculture." <u>J. Farm Economics</u> 44(August, 1962): 679-89.

Coase, Ronald. 1937. "The Nature of the Firm." <u>Economica</u> 4: 386-405.

George Morris Centre Food Industry Research Group. 1993. <u>Alternative Business Linkages: The Case of the Poultry Industry</u>. Guelph, Ontario: George Morris Centre, University of Guelph.

Goldberg, R.A. 1968. <u>Agribusiness Coordination: A System Approach to the Wheat, Soybean and Florida Orange Economies</u>. Boston: Graduate School of Business Administration, Harvard University.

Grimes, Glenn and V.J. Rhodes. 1994. "Marketings of the Nation's Very Large Producers of Hogs." Columbia: University of Missouri Agricultural Economics Report 1994-3.

Hayenga, Marvin, V.J. Rhodes, J.A. Brandt, and R.E. Deiter. 1985. <u>The U.S. Pork Sector: Changing Structure and Organization</u>. Ames: Iowa State University Press.

Hayenga, Marvin, R.D. Duvick, W.G. Bursch, and J.W. Allen. 1972. "An Industry Survey of Coordination in the Pork Industry." <u>Symposium: Vertical Coordination in the Pork Industry,</u> eds. R. Schneidau and L.A. Duewer, Westport, CT: AVI.

Hayenga, M. and K. Kimle. 1992. "Evolution of Producer-Packer Relationships." In <u>Proceedings of the Minnesota Swine Conference for Veterinarians</u>. St. Paul: University of Minnesota Veterinary Continuing Education.

Hayenga, Marvin. 1994. "The Pork Slaughter Industry: Continuing Change." <u>National Hog Farmer</u>, May 15, 1994.

Katz, Michael L. 1989. "Vertical Contractual Relations." <u>Handbook of Industrial Organization,</u> R. Schmalensee and R.D. Willig, eds., New York: North Holland, Vol. 1, pp. 656-721.

Mahoney, J.T. 1992. "The Choice of Organizational Form: Vertical Financial Ownership Versus Other Methods of Vertical Integration." <u>Strategic Management Journal</u>, Vol. 13, pp. 559-84.

Marion, Bruce, editor. 1986. <u>The Organization and Performance of the U.S. Food System</u>. Lexington, Mass.: D. C. Heath.

Mighell, R.L. and L.A. Jones. 1963. <u>Vertical Coordination in Agriculture</u>. AER19. Washington, DC: USDA-ERS.

Perry, Martin K. 1989. "Vertical Integration: Determinants and Effects." <u>Handbook of Industrial Organization</u>, R. Schmalensee and R.D. Willig, eds., New York: North Holland, Vol. 1, pp. 183-255.

Rhodes, V.J., R.M.S. Finley, and G.A. Grimes. 1974. <u>A 1974 Survey of Large-Scale Hog Production in the U.S.</u> Columbia: University of Missouri Extension Special Report 165.

Sauvee, Laic. 1994. "Vertical Coordination in Agribusiness Concepts, Theories and Applications." Department of Agricultural Economics, Purdue University.

Williamson, O.E. 1989. "Transaction Cost Economies." <u>Handbook of Industrial Organization</u>. Volume 1. Eds. R. Schmalensee and R.D. Willig. New York: North Holland.

Williamson, O.E. 1971. "The Vertical Integration of Production: Market Failure Considerations." <u>American Economic Review</u> 61: 112-23.

Appendix I. Survey Forms Used

Introductory Statement for Pork Packer, Feed Company and Large Hog Producer Surveys

I am (identify interviewer). I am surveying the largest (select appropriate one: pork packers; feed companies; hog production contractors/integrators) regarding the changes occurring in the pork industry vertical coordination system. This survey is part of a Congressionally mandated and funded study which we are doing for the Packers and Stockyards Administration, U.S. Department of Agriculture. The survey has been approved by the Office of Management and Budget (Control no.0590-0005 which expires in April 1996).

We need your help in getting a clearer picture of the how the marketing, contracting and ownership linkages between packers, hog production, feed companies and other participants in the pork industry are likely to change, why, and what the implications are for the industry. Your response is voluntary and not required by law. Your responses will be kept confidential and not attributed to you or your company; they will be combined with the other survey responses and other publicly available information in a report which will be reviewed, cleared for publication, and released through the U.S. Department of Agriculture, Packers and Stockyards Administration, and provided to the Congress and the public. When we finish the interview, I'll ask if you would like to get a copy of the report, and ask for your mailing address to put on the USDA mailing list.

With this as background, are you willing to begin with the first question?

Survey of Pork Packers

OMB no. 0590-0005					Expiration date April 1996

Hayenga, Rhodes, Grimes, and Lawrence Partnership is contract agent for Packers & Stockyards Administration, U.S. Department of Agriculture. Response to this survey is voluntary and not required by law. Individual responses will be kept confidential and combined with other responses for the study.

Name of person interviewed:_____
Position in firm:_____
Firm:_____
Address:_____

In 1993, how many slaughter hogs did your firm acquire using the spot market, marketing contracts, production contracts, production in your own facilities or other purchasing or supply methods ? [place no. of head below]

1. spot market purchase							no.hd
    directly from producers:
        at plant or own buying station?				_____
        from terminal or auction markets?				_____
        from dealers or order buyers?				_____
2. marketing contract(s)?
        continuing								_____
        definite contract length						_____
            how long?_____
3. Producing your own hogs in your own or joint
    venture facilities?							_____
4. Producing your own hogs via production
    contract in someone else's facilities?				_____
5. Other [Describe]
    _____					_____
    _____					_____
    _____					_____

2. What was your total 1993 slaughter volume?			_____
   [Add volumes noted above and check consistency]

3. What percentage of your volume do you expect to acquire using each procurement method in 1998?

                                       <u>1998 %</u>

1. Spot market purchase
 directly from producers:
  at plant or own buying station? _____
  from terminal or auction markets? _____
  from dealers or order buyers _____
2. Marketing contract(s)?
  continuing _____
  definite contract length _____
   how long?_____
3. Producing your own hogs in your own or joint venture facilities? _____
4. Producing your own hogs via production contract in someone else's facilities? _____
5. Other [Describe]

 _____ _____
 _____ _____
 _____ _____

[If part of the slaughter supply is not from production or marketing contracts, joint venture or own production, skip to last two questions; if part of their supply is from production or marketing contracts, or joint venture, for each type of arrangement, ask:]

Please describe what each party to the arrangement is to provide and receive (i.e. the important provisions of the contract or venture).
 [Use Schedule A as a checklist to tabulate responses. If more than one type of marketing or production contracts are used, fill out Schedules for each.]

Would you send me a copy of material you have available which outlines or illustrates the key elements of these arrangements (sample contracts, etc.)?

What are the primary reasons for your use of each procurement method used (except spot market and short-term marketing contracts (less than 6 months)), starting with the most important and ending with the least important one worth mentioning.
 [Interviewer will rank the reasons according to importance on Schedule B provided for each arrangement -- 1,2 3, etc.]

Are there any disadvantages to you in using this arrangement?   Yes   No

> [If yes] Which are the major ones, starting with the most important and ending with the least important worth mentioning?
> > [Use Schedule B, and follow similar procedure in tabulating responses.]

What do you consider the major benefits of each arrangement for hog producers, in order of importance? Start with the most important. [Use Schedule C to record rankings.]

What are the major disadvantages for producers, in order of importance? [Use Schedule C to record rankings.]

What do you expect to be the major changes in the ways packers will be linked to hog production or producers five years from now? Why?

1. _____
2. _____
3. _____
4. _____

What key problems or benefits would you expect from these changes for the pork industry?

1. _____
2. _____
3. _____
4. _____

Would you like a copy of the final report sent to you?   Yes   No

Schedule A. Provisions of Contracts or Joint Ventures

Circle appropriate coordination arrangement:

Production contract   Marketing contract   Joint venture

Packer requires/producer provides   Check those indicated
    minimum volume   _____
    minimum quality   _____
    type or source of feed used   _____
    breeding type/source   _____
    type of facilities   _____
    time length of arrangement   _____
    other, please specify _____   _____
                              _____

Resources provided by packer
    breeding stock   _____
    feeder pigs   _____
    feed   _____
    credit/loan assistance   _____
    veterinary services   _____
    management services   _____
    other, please specify _____   _____
                              _____

Pricing or fee arrangement(s)
    Fee   fixed: per head   _____
                     per day   _____
                     other _____   _____
        with incentives, related to:
            death loss   _____
            feed efficiency   _____
            production cost   _____
            profits per head   _____
            other _____
    Pricing arrangement
        fixed price   _____
        (carcass merit related?)   _____
        formula price, based on
        _____
        (carcass merit related?)   _____
        fixed profit per head or cwt.   _____
        profit target or range, based on
        _____
        other, please specify _____   _____

Schedule B. Reasons for Use/Disadvantages

(List will not be read to respondent)

Circle correct procurement/coordination method:

| Marketing Cntrct | Production cntrct | Joint ven | Own prod |

Reasons for use
Ranking   Comments
____increased volume of hogs
____lower volume risk
____improved quality of product
____less quality risk/variability
____improved scheduling
____improved plant efficiency
____rivals use it/keep up with them
____reduced transaction cost
____reduced hog production cost
____forestall rivals access to these suppliers
____reduced price risk
____increased profits
____other, please specify   _____
____   _____

Disadvantages
____lower volume of hogs
____increased volume risk
____inadequate quality of product
____too much quality risk/variability
____scheduling difficulty
____lower plant efficiency
____rivals foreclose access to good suppliers
____higher transaction cost
____increased hog production cost
____rivals programs difficult to compete with
____higher prices paid
____higher price variability/risk
____lower profits
____other, please specify   _____
____   _____

Can you estimate the amount of net benefit, if any, in $/head or cwt, for this arrangement compared to the spot market purchase at your buying station or plant? _____

Schedule C. Major Benefits/Disadvantages for Hog Producers
(List will not be read to respondent)

67

Circle correct procurement/coordination method:

Marketing Cntrct   Production cntrct   Joint venture

Benefits

Ranking   Comments
____increased facility and labor utilization
____reduced price risk
____improved genetics supplied
____increased capital available
____improved technology provided
____management services provided
____lower financial risk
____reduced hog production cost
____assured access to market outlets
____increased profits
____lower transaction cost
____other, please specify   _____
____   _____

Disadvantages

Ranking
____don't keep facilities full
____increased disease/death risk
____inadequate quality of hogs
____inadequate payment for services/facilities
____disagreements regarding contract
       or joint venture obligations
____management services inadequate
____reduced independence
____reduced flexibility
____increased hog production cost
____lower profits
____other, please specify   _____
____   _____
____   _____

SURVEY OF PORK PRODUCERS

OMB No. 0590-0005	Expiration Date: April 1996
Hayenga, Rhodes, Grimes, and Lawrence, Partnership is contract agent for Packers & Stockyards Administration U.S. Department of Agriculture	Response to this survey is voluntary and not required by law. Individual responses will be kept confidential and combined with other responses for the study.

Name of person interviewed _____

Position in firm _____

Name of firm _____

Address of firm headquarters _____

_____

1. List the major livestock species your firm marketed in 1993 and the approximate numbers of each:

Commodity	Quantity (no. of head)
Slaughter hogs	_____
Feeder pigs	_____
Swine breeding stock	_____
Beef cattle	_____
Other _____	_____

2. List the states in which you marketed pigs/hogs in 1993 and the approximate percentage of your total head sold in each:

State	Percentage of Volume (should total to 100)
_____	_____
_____	_____
_____	_____
_____	_____
_____	_____

3. What percent of the slaughter hogs that you marketed to packers in 1993 were by these methods:

   (a) What would you expect those percentages to be in 1998?

			1993	1998
(1)	Transaction at delivery (spot)		%	%
(2)	Forward contracts prior to delivery		%	%
(3)	Under a production contract or joint venture of the packer		%	%
(4)	Other (specify _____)		%	%
			$\Sigma = 100$	

   _____

   _____

4. <u>If you reported use of forward market contracts in 1993</u>, *(otherwise skip to q. 5).*

   (a) What % of those forward contract hogs were sold at a base price fixed 15 days or more before delivery? _____ %

   (b) What % were priced using a formula price? _____ %

       (1) explain the type of formula used _____

   _____

   _____

   _____

   (c) What % were priced by a different technique? _____ %

                                                                                                                                                 $\Sigma = 100$

       (1) explain the pricing technique used _____

   _____

   _____

   _____

   (d) Are these forward contracts written or verbal? _____

(e) Are these forward contracts for a fixed period or do they continue until canceled by either party? _____

    (1) if for a fixed period, how long? _____

4. (f) Does the packer require: (check)

    ____ approved breeding stock
    ____ minimal quality standards of all deliveries
    ____ minimal volume per delivery or per period
    ____ delivery at a specific time of day or day of week

    (1) *For each item checked, obtain details of the requirements.*
    _____
    _____

(g) How many packers do you currently have forward contracts with? ___ One ___ > One

(h) Beginning with the most important, what are the benefits to you of this forward contract arrangement? *(Rank) [Interviewer will use this and ensuing lists to record the open ended responses to each question. Lists will not be read to respondent.]*

    ____ (1) reduces price risk
    ____ (2) better prices for hogs
    ____ (3) assures market outlet for hogs
    ____ (4) reduces transaction costs and efforts
    ____ (5) improves ability to get credit
    ____ (6) facilitates expansion
    ____ (7) improved genetics supplied
    ____ (8) increased profits
    ____ (9) other (specify) _____
    _____
    _____
    _____

(I) Beginning with the most important, what are the costs and problems to you? *(Rank)*

    ____ A. NONE
    ____ (1) lower returns
    ____ (2) unanticipated transaction problems
    ____ (3) unanticipated disputes regarding agreement
    ____ (4) prevents shopping for better bids
    ____ (5) reduced independence
    ____ (6) inadequate genetics
    ____ (7) doesn't pay for the inconvenience

____ (8) reduced flexibility
____ (9) other (specify) _____
_____
_____

(j) What do you believe are the benefits to the packer of this forward contract arrangement?
(Rank)

____ (1) secures regular supply of hogs
____ (2) lower buying costs
____ (3) may increase volume of hogs
____ (4) obtain better quality hogs
____ (5) improved scheduling
____ (6) forestall rivals access to hogs
____ (7) increased profits
____ (8) other (specify) _____
_____
_____
_____

4. (k) What do you believe are the costs or disadvantages to the packer of this forward contract?
(Rank)

____ A. NONE
____ (1) possibly pay higher prices at times
____ (2) takes extra market price risks
____ (3) loses some flexibility of operations
____ (4) additional management problems
____ (5) increased volume risk
____ (6) inadequate quality
____ (7) high transaction costs
____ (8) rivals programs difficult to compete with
____ (9) lower profits
____ (10) other (specify) _____
_____
_____

5. **If you reported a joint venture or contract production of a packer's hogs:**

    (a)   What % of those contract hogs were on a profit share or joint venture basis? _____ %

    (b)   What % of those contract hogs were on a per head fee (with or without premiums or discounts)? _____ %

    (c)   What % of those contract hogs were under some other payment plan?
(Specify _____) _____ %
$\Sigma = 100$

    (d)   What packer(s) has this production contract? _____

    (e)   How long has this contract been in effect? _____

    (f)   Is this production contract for a fixed period or does it continue until canceled by either side? _____

        (1)   If for a fixed period, how long? _____

    (g)   Beginning with the most important, what are the benefits to you of this production contract arrangement? *(Rank)*

        _____ (1) reduces price risk
        _____ (2) simplifies management
        _____ (3) assures outlet for hogs
        _____ (4) reduces transaction costs and efforts
        _____ (5) improves ability to get credit
        _____ (6) facilitates expansion
        _____ (7) improved genetics
        _____ (8) increased profits
        _____ (9) other (specify) _____

(h) Beginning with the most important, what are the costs and problems to you of this production contract? *(Rank)*

- _____ (1) lower returns
- _____ (2) unanticipated transaction problems
- _____ (3) unanticipated disputes regarding agreement
- _____ (4) don't keep facilities full
- _____ (5) reduced independence
- _____ (6) poor quality inputs
- _____ (7) other (specify) _____

_____
_____
_____

5. (I) Beginning with the most important, what are the benefits to the packer of this production contract arrangement? *(Rank)*

- _____ (1) secures regular supply of hogs
- _____ (2) lower procurement costs
- _____ (3) may increase volume of hogs
- _____ (4) obtain better quality hogs
- _____ (5) profitable production
- _____ (6) improved scheduling
- _____ (7) other (specify) _____

_____
_____
_____

(j) Beginning with the most important, what are the costs or disadvantages to the packer of this production contract? *(Rank)*

- _____ (1) hogs cost more at times
- _____ (2) takes extra market price risks
- _____ (3) loses some flexibility of operations
- _____ (4) additional management problems
- _____ (5) unprofitable production
- _____ (6) takes more capital
- _____ (7) other (specify) _____

_____
_____
_____

6. Do you have contracts, joint ventures, or other continuing arrangements with one or more commercial feed companies?

   _____ Yes _____ No *(If no skip to q. 8)*

   (If yes). Do these arrangements include? (check)

   _____ (a) feed company finances the hog feed
   _____ (b) feed company finances more than the hog feed

   (1) What else does it finance? _____

   _____

   _____

   _____ (c) feed is provided at a negotiated, favorable price
   _____ (d) feed and hogs provided under contract production

6. (e) specify any other kinds of arrangements _____

   _____

   _____

   _____

   (f) how long has each of these arrangements been in effect? *(record after h)*

   (g) what volume of hogs was covered by each of these arrange-ments in 1993? *(record after h)*

(h) do any of these arrangements give the feed company influence over hog marketing decisions?

	Arrangements				
	a	b	c	d	e
(f) How long in effect (mon.)	___	___	___	___	___
(g) Volume of hogs (no.)	___	___	___	___	___
(h) Marketing influence? (yes or no)	___	___	___	___	___

If yes, explain _____

_____

_____

_____

(I) If you have feed company financing, what are the benefits to you beginning with the most important? *(Rank)* *(If no financing, skip to question 6m.)*

    ____ (1) often more credit than available elsewhere
    ____ (2) obtain better credit terms than available elsewhere
    ____ (3) obtain better feed company service
    ____ (4) obtain better feed prices
    ____ (5) other (specify) _____

_____

_____

6. (j) If you have feed company financing, what are the costs and disadvantages to you beginning with the most important? *(Rank)*

    ____ (1) higher than market interest rates
    ____ (2) higher feed costs
    ____ (3) loss of flexibility
    ____ (4) poorer feed company service
    ____ (5) tied to an arrangement that could go sour
    ____ (6) other (specify) _____

_____

_____

(k) If you have feed company financing, what do you believe are the benefits to the feed company beginning with the most important? *(Rank)*

    ____ (1) sells more feed
    ____ (2) gets higher price for feed
    ____ (3) profitable
    ____ (4) other (specify) _____

_____

_____

_____

(l) If you have feed company financing, what do you believe are the costs and disadvantages to the feed company beginning with the most important? *(Rank)*

    ____ (1) greater capital requirements
    ____ (2) more capital at risk
    ____ (3) expensive way to sell feed
    ____ (4) loss of flexibility
    ____ (5) greater management problems
    ____ (6) other (specify) _____

_____

_____

_____

(m) What is (are) the name(s) of the feed company(s)?

_____

_____

7. If you have a production contract or joint venture with a feed company, what are the benefits to you? *(If no such arrange-ments, skip to question 8.)*

    ____ (1) reduces price risk
    ____ (2) better prices for hogs
    ____ (3) assures outlet for hogs
    ____ (4) reduces transaction costs and efforts
    ____ (5) improves ability to get credit

____ (6) facilitates expansion
____ (7) other (specify) _____

_____

_____

_____

(a) What are the costs and disadvantages to you of contract production for a feed company beginning with the most important?

____ (1) lower returns
____ (2) unanticipated transaction problems
____ (3) unanticipated disputes regarding agreement
____ (4) don't keep facilities full
____ (5) reduced independence
____ (6) poor quality inputs
____ (7) other (specify) _____

_____

_____

_____

(b) What do you believe are the advantages for the feed company of contract production beginning with the most important?

____ (1) sells more feed
____ (2) profitable
____ (3) positions feed company as a key player in the "new" hog industry
____ (4) obtains helpful expertise of others
____ (5) obtains economies of size
____ (4) other (specify) _____

_____

_____

_____

7. (c) What do you believe are the costs and disadvantages to the feed company of contract production beginning with the most important?

    ____ (1) may incur financial losses (poor returns)
    ____ (2) incur greater market risks
    ____ (3) complicates management
    ____ (4) loses some flexibility of operations
    ____ (5) takes more capital
    ____ (6) unanticipated transactional problems
    ____ (7) other (specify) _____

_____

_____

_____

8. Do you have contracts with one or more growers to farrow or to finish pigs for you?

    _____ Yes   _____ No *(If no, skip to question 9)*

(a) Of the hogs you marketed in 1993, what percent were finished by growers?

    _____

(If none, skip to question 9)

(b) Are your finishing contracts? *(Read the list and check the ones applying.)*

    ____ (1) profit share
    ____ (2) fee per head marketed
    ____ (3) other (specify) _____

_____

_____

_____

(c) If more than one type of finishing contract, what is the relative volume of each?

    (1) _____ %
    (2) _____ %
    (3) _____ %
           $\Sigma = 100$

8. (d) Beginning with the most important, what are the benefits to you of contract finishing? *(Rank)*

   _____ (1) facilitates expansion
   _____ (2) supplements available capital
   _____ (3) profitable
   _____ (4) good community relations
   _____ (5) acquires highly motivated producers
   _____ (6) other (specify) _____

   _____

   _____

   _____

   (e) Beginning with the most important, what are the costs, risks, and disadvantages to you of contract finishing? *(Rank)*

   _____ (1) higher costs and lower returns
   _____ (2) more risks
   _____ (3) more management problems
   _____ (4) bad community relations
   _____ (5) less efficient production
   _____ (6) poorer quality hogs
   _____ (7) other (specify) _____

   _____

   _____

   _____

   (f) Beginning with the most important, what are the benefits to your typical grower? *(Rank)*

   _____ (1) reduced price risks
   _____ (2) more certain returns
   _____ (3) allows producers to get started or facilitates expansion
   _____ (4) more income or better cash flow
   _____ (5) simplifies management
   _____ (6) supplemental income
   _____ (7) other (specify) _____

   _____

8. (g) Beginning with the most important, what are the costs, risks, and disadvantages of contract production for your typical grower? *(Rank)*

   ____ (1) eliminates chance of big returns
   ____ (2) less independence
   ____ (3) risk of losing contract
   ____ (4) other (specify) _____

   _____

   _____

   _____

   (h) Beginning with the most important, what are the charac-teristics that you look for in a prospective grower? *(Rank)*

   ____ (1) hog experience
   ____ (2) willingness to learn
   ____ (3) energetic and hard-working
   ____ (4) dependability
   ____ (5) good references
   ____ (6) good character
   ____ (7) sufficient equity to finance facilities
   ____ (8) has other job to provide income
   ____ (9) will work full-time at production
   ____ (10) other (specify) _____

   _____

   _____

   _____

9. Of your slaughter hog marketings in 1993, what percent of the feeder pigs originated from these sources?

    (1) your own facilities _____ %
    (2) produced by contract growers _____ %
    (3) purchased from others _____ %
    (4) other (specify _____) _____ %
    $\Sigma = 100$

_____

_____

_____

(If none produced by contract, skip to question 10)

9. (a) Of your pig production contracts, what percent are:

    (1) profit share _____ %
    (2) fee per head of pigs delivered _____ %
    (3) Other (specify _____) _____ %
    $\Sigma = 100$

_____

_____

_____

(b) Beginning with the most important, what are the benefits to you of contract pig production? *(Rank)*

    ____ (1) facilitates expansion
    ____ (2) supplements available capital
    ____ (3) profitable
    ____ (4) good community relations
    ____ (5) acquires highly motivated producers
    ____ (6) improved or healthier pigs
    ____ (7) lower costs than can buy
    ____ (8) assured supply of pigs
    ____ (9) other (specify) _____

_____

_____

(c) Beginning with the most important, what are the costs, risks, and disadvantages to you of contract pig production? *(Rank)*

	____ (1) higher costs and/or lower returns
	____ (2) more production and/or price risks
	____ (3) more management problems
	____ (4) bad community relations
	____ (5) less efficient production
	____ (6) poorer quality pigs
	____ (7) other (specify) _____

	_____

	_____

9. (d) What do you perceive as the benefits of contract pig production to your typical grower beginning with the most important? *(Rank)*

	____ (1) reduced price risks
	____ (2) more certain returns
	____ (3) allows producers to get started or facilities expansion
	____ (4) more income or better cash flow
	____ (5) simplifies management
	____ (6) other (specify) _____

	_____

	_____

(e) What do you perceive as the costs, risks, and disadvan-tages of contract pig production to the growers beginning with the most important? *(Rank)*

	____ (1) eliminates chance of big returns
	____ (2) less independence
	____ (3) risk of losing contract
	____ (4) other (specify) _____

	_____

	_____

(f) Beginning with the most important, what are the charac-teristics that you look for in a prospective contract pig producer? *(Rank)*

    _____ (1) hog experience
    _____ (2) willingness to learn
    _____ (3) energetic and hard-working
    _____ (4) dependability
    _____ (5) good references
    _____ (6) good character
    _____ (7) sufficient equity to finance facilities
    _____ (8) has other job to provide income
    _____ (9) will work full-time at production
    _____ (10) other (specify) _____

    _____

    _____

    _____

10. Do you have any contractual or continuing arrangements with sellers of breeding stock? *(If no, skip to question 11)*

    (a) What volumes of gilts and boars were purchased in 1993 through these arrangements?

        _____ gilts
        _____ boars

    (b) Do you have a contract for a fixed period or does the arrangement continue until canceled by either party?
        _____

        (1) If for a fixed period, how long? _____

    (c) Did you purchase breeding stock in 1993 from more than one seller? ____ Yes ____ No

11. In your opinion, what will be the major change in the next five years in who produces hogs and how feed companies relate to producers and packers. Why?

    (1) _____

        _____

    (2) _____

        _____

(3) _____

_____

(a) What key benefits and problems will result for large producers like yourself from these expected changes?

(1) _____

_____

(2) _____

_____

(3) _____

_____

12. What volume of marketings of hogs/pigs do you project for this firm for 1998?

_____

If you would like a copy of the final report, what mailing address should we forward to the USDA?

SURVEY OF LARGE FEED COMPANIES

OMB No. 0590-0005	Expiration Date: April 1996
Hayenga, Rhodes, Grimes and Lawrence, Partnership is contract agent for Packers & Stockyards Administration U.S. Department of Agriculture	Response to this survey is voluntary and not required by law. Individual responses will be kept confidential and combined with other responses for the study.

Name of person interviewed _____

Position in firm _____

Name of firm _____

Address of firm headquarters _____

_____

1. Does your firm produce feed for hogs? ___ Yes ___ No
   (If no, terminate interview.)

2. In 1993, what was the approximate tonnage of hog feed produced by your firm and what percentage was it of your total feed tonnage for all livestock and poultry?

   _____ tons _____ % *(If less than 15,000 tons, terminate interview.)*

3. In 1993 what percentages of your hog feed were:

   _____ sold through normal channels without credit extension to buyers
   _____ sold through a program financing the feed (perhaps financing more)
   _____ fed to your own hogs in own or leased facilities
   _____ fed to your hogs in grower facilities (production contract)
   _____ fed to hogs jointly owned with packers or investors
   _____ other (specify) _____
   $\Sigma=100$

   _____

   _____

   _____

4. *(Ask, if some feed is sold through a feed financing program.)*

(a) Is your financing (check)?

    ___ of feed only
    ___ feed plus some other variable inputs
    ___ feed plus a loan (or a loan guarantee) on facilities
    ___ other (specify) _____

_____

_____

_____

(b) Is your financing on a continuing or long-term basis or on a specific group of hogs?

(c) Is your financing a verbal understanding or a formal, written agreement?

(d) Is your financing tied to use of a (1) specific quality of breeding stock or (2) to a specific genetic line?

    ___ Yes to (1)   ___ Yes to (2)   ___ No to both

(e) Does your financing allow you to specify when, how or where the slaughter hogs are marketed? ___ Yes ___ No

If yes, in what way? _____

(f) Beginning with the most important, what are the benefits to you of this financing agreement? *(If company used more than one financing arrangement, ask this and questions g to I for each.)* Rank each mentioned on list F1. *[Interviewer will use this and ensuing lists to record the open ended responses to each question. Lists will not be read to the respondent.]*

(g) Beginning with the most important, what are the costs and disadvantages to you of a financing program? *Rank each on list F2.*

(h) Beginning with the most important, what do you perceive are the benefits to the producer of a financing program? *Rank each on list F3.*

(I) Beginning with the most important, what do you perceive are the costs and disadvantages to producers of a financing program? *Rank each on list F4.*

(j) Do you expect to expand the volume of feed sold by these arrangements? ___ Yes ___ No

(k) Which, if any, of these finance arrangements do you think will increase in industry use in the next five years?

_____

_____

_____

5. *(Ask, if according to q. 3 some feed is fed by contract growers.)*

   (a) How many slaughter hogs did you market in 1993 from your contract production?
   _____

   (b) How many slaughter hogs do you expect to market in 1994 from your contract production? _____

   (If less than 10,000 for each year, skip to question 6.)

   (c) Of those hogs, what percent were farrowed by your contract growers?
   _____

(d) In what states are these contract operations? _____

_____

_____

_____

_____

(e) Do your contract growers include anyone marketing <u>less -than</u> 1,000 head per year?___ Yes___ No

5. (f) Of your finishing contracts:

    (1) What percent of those contract hogs were on a per head fee (with or without incentives) _____%

    (2) What percent of those contract hogs were on a profit/loss sharing arrangement _____%

    (3) What percent of those contract hogs were under some other payment plan _____%

$\Sigma = 100$

(specify)_____

_____

_____

_____

(g) How long have you been engaged in contract hog production?
_____

(h) Are your production contracts for a fixed period or do they continue until canceled by either party? _____

_____

    (1) If for a fixed period, how long for farrowing and how long for finishing?

        _____ months farrowing
        _____ months finishing

(I) Beginning with the most important, what are the benefits of your contract production of hogs? *(Rank each men-tioned on list F1.)*

(j) Beginning with the most important, what are the costs and disadvantages to you of contract production of hogs? *(Rank each on list F2.)*

(k) Beginning with the most important, what are the benefits to the grower of contract production of hogs? *(Rank each on list F3.)*

(l) Beginning with the most important, what are the costs and disadvantages to the grower of contract production of hogs? *(Rank each on list F4.)*

6. (a) Do you have joint ventures with:

   ___ packers
   ___ investors
   ___ super-producers (over 50,000 marketed per year)
   ___ other (specify) _____

   If joint ventures with packers, what are their names?

   _____

   (b) How many slaughter hogs were marketed in 1993 from your joint venture(s)?
   _____

   How many slaughter hogs do you expect to market in 1994 from your joint venture(s)?
   _____

   (If less than 10,000 head for each year, skip to question 7).

   (c) Do these joint ventures involve you doing any more than providing the feed and sharing in the earnings/losses?

   ___ Yes   ___ No *(If no, skip to 6e.)*

   (d) Do these joint ventures involve a joint sharing of:

   the investment in facilities?   ___ Yes   ___ No

   day to day management decisions?   ___ Yes   ___ No

(e) Beginning with the most important, what are the benefits to you of joint venture hog production? *(Rank each on list F1.)*

(f) Beginning with the most important, what are the costs/ disadvantages to you of joint venture hog production? *(Rank each on list F2.)*

(g) Beginning with the most important, what are the benefits to the other owners of a joint venture with you? *(Rank each on list F5.)*

(h) Beginning with the most important, what are the costs/ disadvantages to other owners of a joint venture with you? *(Rank each on list F6.)*

(I) In what states are these operations? _____

_____

7. *(Ask these questions if company said in q. 3 that it produces any hogs/pigs directly in its own or leased facilities staffed by its own employees.)*

   (a) How many slaughter hogs did you market in 1993 from your own facilities?
   _____

   (b) How many slaughter hogs did you expect to market in 1994 from your own facilities?
   _____

   (If less than 10,000 head for each year, skip to q. 8.)

   (c) In what states are these slaughter hogs marketed? _____

   _____

   _____

   _____

   (d) How long has your company been producing its own hogs/ pigs?
   _____

91

(e) What percentage of your own slaughter hogs:

    ___ (1) were farrowed in your own or leased facilities
    ___ (2) were farrowed by your contract growers
    ___ (3) were purchased as feeder pigs from others
    ___ (4) were obtained as feeder pigs in some other way
$\Sigma=100$ (specify) _____

_____

(f) Beginning with the most important, what are the benefits to you of producing your own slaughter hogs? *(Rank)*

    ___ (1) profitable as an enterprise
    ___ (2) uses more feed and keeps mills busy
    ___ (3) is a by-product of our breeding stock produc-tion
    ___ (4) provides us good experience in case the industry trends in this direction
    ___ (5) other (specify) _____

_____

_____

7. (g) Beginning with the most important, what are the costs and disadvantages to you of producing your own slaughter hogs? *(Rank)*

    ___ (1) less profitable than other enterprises
    ___ (2) complicates management
    ___ (3) offends some customers
    ___ (4) chance of bad public relations
    ___ (5) possible air or water pollution problems
    ___ (6) requires more capital
    ___ (7) other (specify) _____

_____

_____

(h) How much do you expect direct hog production by all feed companies to change in the next 5 years?

    _____ %   up or down? _____

8. Do you have any contractual or continuing arrangements with sellers of breeding stock? ___ Yes ___ No

    (If no, skip to q. 9)

    (a) What volumes of gilts and boars were purchased in 1993 through these arrangements?

    _____ gilts
    _____ boars

    (b) Do you have a contract for a fixed period or does the arrangement continue until canceled by either party?

    _____

    _____

    (1) If for a fixed period, how long? _____

    (c) Did you purchase breeding stock in 1993 from more than one seller? ___ Yes ___ No

9. For hogs that your company markets, or influences the marketing, do you have any continuing or long-term marketing arrangements with packers? ___ Yes ___ No

    (If no, skip to question 10.)

    (a) What are the key provisions of this (these) marketing arrangement(s)? *(Check on packer schedule A.) (If arrangements are strictly spot market or short-term for a specific batch, skip to question 10.)*

    (b) What are the primary reasons for your use of this (these) marketing arrangement(s) starting with the most important and ending with the least important. *(Rank each on list F7.)*

    (c) Are there any disadvantages in these marketing arrangements? ___ Yes ___ No

    (If no, skip to question 10.)

(1) Starting with the most important, what are the major disadvantages. *(Rank each on list.)*

　　___ (1) lower returns
　　___ (2) unanticipated transaction problems
　　___ (3) unanticipated disputes regarding agreement
　　___ (4) prevents shopping for better bids
　　___ (5) reduced independence
　　___ (6) other (specify) _____

　　_____

　　_____

10. In your opinion, what will be the major change in the next five years in who produces hogs and how feed companies relate to producers and packers. Why?

　　(1) _____

　　(2) _____

　　(3) _____

　　(4) _____

10. (a) What key benefits and problems will result for feed companies from these expected changes?

　　(1) _____

　　(2) _____

　　(3) _____

11. What volume of marketings of hogs/pigs do you project for this firm for 1998?

　　_____

If you would like a copy of the final report, what mailing address should we forward to the USDA?

LISTS

F1 Benefits to feed company

     ___ (1) sells more feed
     ___ (2) obtain higher price for feed
     ___ (3) profitable
     ___ (4) positions the company for the future
     ___ (5) obtains expertise of others
     ___ (6) obtains economies of size
     ___ (7) other (specify) _____
                                      _____
                                      _____

F2 costs and disadvantages to feed company

     ___ (1) requires more capital
     ___ (2) increases risks
     ___ (3) increases management problems
     ___ (4) increases expense of selling feed
     ___ (5) reduces flexibility
     ___ (6) unanticipated contract disputes
     ___ (7) lower profit than other uses of capital
     ___ (8) other (specify) _____

F3 Benefits to producers

     ___ (1) often more credit than available elsewhere
     ___ (2) obtain better credit terms than available elsewhere
     ___ (3) obtain better feed company service
     ___ (4) obtain better feed prices
     ___ (5) allows expansion of hog production
     ___ (6) obtain better pigs or breeding stock
     ___ (7) obtain management assistance
     ___ (8) other (specify) _____

F4 Costs and disadvantages to producers

      ___   (1)   higher than market interest rates
      ___   (2)   higher feed costs
      ___   (3)   loss of flexibility
      ___   (4)   poorer feed company service
      ___   (5)   tied to an arrangement that could go sour
      ___   (6)   receive poor quality or sick pigs
      ___   (7)   don't keep facilities full
      ___   (8)   inadequate returns
      ___   (9)   other (specify) _____

F5   Benefits to other owners

      ___   (1)   obtains expertise
      ___   (2)   reduces transaction costs
      ___   (3)   profitable
      ___   (4)   positions them for growth
      ___   (5)   obtains economies of size
      ___   (6)   facilitates borrowing
      ___   (7)   other (specify) _____

F6   Costs and disadvantages to other owners

      ___   (1)   increases risks
      ___   (2)   complicates management
      ___   (3)   reduces flexibility of operations
      ___   (4)   may incur poor returns (or losses)
      ___   (5)   forces a sharing of managerial control
      ___   (6)   may be unanticipated disputes
      ___   (7)   other (specify) _____

F7   Reasons for marketing arrangements with packer

    ____ (1) reduces price risk
    ____ (2) better prices for hogs
    ____ (3) assures market outlet for hogs
    ____ (4) reduces transaction costs and efforts
    ____ (5) improves ability to get credit
    ____ (6) facilitates expansion
    ____ (7) improved genetics supplied
    ____ (8) increased profit
    ____ (9) other (specify) _____

The United States Department of Agriculture (USDA) prohibits discrimination in its programs on the basis of race, color, national origin, sex, religion, age, disability, political beliefs, and marital or familial status. (Not all prohibited bases apply to all programs.) Persons with disabilities who require alternative means for communications of program information (braille, large print, audiotape, etc.) should contact the USDA Office of Communications at (202) 720-2791.

To file a complaint, write the Secretary of Agriculture, U.S. Department of Agriculture, Washington, DC 20250, or call (202) 720-7327 (voice) or (202) 720-1127 (TDD). USDA is an equal employment opportunity employer.

www.ingramcontent.com/pod-product-compliance
Lightning Source LLC
Chambersburg PA
CBHW081136170526
45165CB00008B/2699